Mastering
Marketing

HSC Business Studies Topic 2

Graham Roll

This book is dedicated to the late Mike Lembach —
friend, colleague & mentor.

Five Senses Education Pty Ltd
2/195 Prospect Highway
Seven Hills 2147
New South Wales
Australia

Roll, Graham
Mastering Marketing HSC Business Studies Topic 2
ISBN 978-1-74130-981-2

Contents

Marketing   **5**

  2.1 The role of marketing   **9**

  2.2 Influences on marketing   **23**

  2.3 The marketing process   **39**

  2.4 Marketing strategies   **57**

Glossary   **87**

Rationale

This is a student topic book. Its purpose is to provide a concise, yet comprehensive coverage of the Marketing topic in the HSC Course. Students are advised to seek other references and case studies in this topic because it is important to read as widely as possible in order to get the most from your study of the topic.

As far as possible, the material is presented in the same order as the Board of Studies syllabus.

This book includes a syllabus outline with Board of Studies outcomes together with the "learn to" aspects of the topic. Students are reminded that assessment task in Business Studies will always relate to syllabus topics and outcomes.

For case studies, students may find that useful information may be obtained by contacting the various chambers of commerce in addition to government departments and by using the internet which will give you up to date information in this area. Indeed, students who are aiming to maximise their performance in Business Studies should research these web sites and read newspaper articles for the most up to date facts and figures.

Topic 2

MARKETING

The focus of this topic is to study the main elements involved in the development and implementation of successful marketing strategies.

Overview of Content and Outcomes

There are **four** major areas to be covered in this topic and they are as follows:
- The role of marketing
- Influences on marketing
- The marketing process
- Marketing strategies.

2.1 The Role of Marketing

- The strategic role of marketing goods and services
- The interdependence with other key business functions
- Production, selling and marketing approaches
- Types of markets: resource, industrial, intermediate, consumer, mass, niche

2.2 Influences on Marketing

- Factors influencing customer choice: psychological, sociocultural, economic, government
- Consumer laws such as deceptive and misleading advertising, price discrimination, implied conditions and warranties
- Ethical aspects: truth, accuracy and good taste in advertising, products that may damage health, engaging in fair competition, sugging.

2.3 The Marketing Process

- Situational analysis: SWOT, product life cycle
- Market research
- Establishing market objectives
- Identifying target markets
- Developing marketing strategies
- Implementation, monitoring and controlling: developing a financial forecast, comparing actual and planned results, revising the marketing strategy.

2.4 Marketing Strategies

▪ Market segmentation, product/service differentiation and positioning

▪ Products: goods and/or services including branding and packaging.

▪ Price including pricing methods: cost pricing, market pricing and competition based pricing:
  - pricing strategies such as skimming, penetration pricing, loss leaders and price points
  - price and quality interaction.

▪ Promotion:
  – elements of the promotion mix such as advertising, personal selling and relationship marketing, sales promotions, publicity and public relations
  – the communication process i.e. opinion leaders and word of mouth

▪ Place/distribution:
  – distribution channels
  – channel choice: intensive, selective, exclusive
  – physical distribution issues: transport, warehousing, inventory

▪ People, processes and physical evidence

▪ e-marketing

▪ Global marketing:
  – global branding
  – standardisation
  – customisation
  – global pricing
  – competitive positioning.

Outcomes

The **10 outcomes** for this topic are to:
- critically analyse the role of business in Australia and globally
- evaluate management strategies in response to changes in internal and external influences
- discuss the social and ethical responsibilities of management
- analyse business functions and processes in large global businesses
- explain management strategies and their impact on business
- evaluate the effectiveness of management in the performance of business
- plan and conduct investigations into contemporary business practices
- organise and evaluate information for actual and hypothetical business situations
- communicate business information, issues and concepts in appropriate formats
- apply mathematical concepts appropriately in business situations.

Also important to the understanding of your syllabus content is the section of the syllabus known as the **'learn to'** components of the topic.

Here you are being asked to **examine contemporary business issues** in order to be able to:
- explain why goods and/or services are central to both marketing and operations
- examine why ethical behaviour and government regulation are important in marketing
- assess why a mix of promotional strategies is important in the marketing of goods and services.

You are also being asked to **investigate aspects of business using hypothetical situations and actual business case studies to:**
- evaluate the marketing strategies for a good or service
- analyse a marketing plan for a business
- explain how globalisation has affected marketing management.

2.1 The Role of Marketing

Business Strategic planning

This involves:
- defining the company mission
- setting company goals and objectives
- designing the product
- planning the marketing strategies.

Management must continually ask:
- What is our business?
- Who are our customers?
- How can we best serve our customers best now?
- How can we best serve our customers best in the future?

The strategic role of marketing

Marketing is not simply "advertising". It is a combination of things, usually referred to the 4Ps :
- Product: the way it is presented
- Price: the way it is priced
- Promotion: the advertising of the product or service
- Place: where the product is sold and how it is distributed to the customer.

Marketing is the **strategic** heart of the business plan. Strategic provisions have a 3-5 year perspective. The marketing strategy will be consistent with the other elements of the business plan. It will encompass the overall aims and objectives of the business in terms of philosophy, ethics, output and profit. A sound marketing plan will ensure the business knows and understands its position in the market place, who its target market is, how to promote its product most effectively and how best to deal with its competition.

In most businesses undertaking any form of marketing, there are a large number of specialists involved in the process, including market researchers, research and development personnel, financial analysts, factory staff, advertising consultants and sales personnel. The marketing plan must coordinate all of these people at the operational level so that the overall strategic goals of the business are met.

N.B. Operational planning involves making decisions about which groups or departments will be responsible for carrying out the various elements of the strategic plan and decides what needs to be done, when, by whom and at what cost.

The role of marketing is to coordinate the efforts of all these personnel, directing them towards common goals:

- **Maximise sales and therefore consumption and profits.** Marketing managers will try to maximise consumer purchasing in order to increase the profits of the business.
- **Increase market penetration and market share.** By this we mean more people buying the product and having a greater share of the available market for the product. It is expressed as a percentage of the available market for the product. For example if the total market is 100%, the share held by company X might be 6.5%.
- **Maximise consumer choice.** By marketing a product consumer choice is maximised when consumers find those goods that precisely satisfy their wants. Car manufacturers provide customers with the opportunity to purchase the model that suits them. For example the number of doors, engine size, colour, interior, optional extras such as sun roof, satellite navigation etc.

However some argue that maximising consumer choice comes at a cost. You can agree or disagree with these points.

Firstly, goods and services will become more expensive, since greater variety means smaller production runs. Higher prices will reduce consumers' real income and therefore consumption. Secondly, the increase in product variety will require greater consumer search and effort. Thirdly, more products will not necessarily increase the consumers' real choice. For example there are many brands of laundry detergent in supermarkets in Australia and all of them get the washing clean. Indeed surveys have shown that consumers are not any more happy or satisfied when there are many brands of the same thing to choose from. When a product category contains many brands with few differences this is called proliferation.

- **Maximise consumer satisfaction:** the customer will want more. This theory asserts that by consuming more, the customer will be happier. However there is no real way of measuring levels of satisfaction through the consumption of more goods. Also, the amount of satisfaction one receives from consuming more goods is related to the number of other people who have similar goods.
- **Maximise life quality:** This theory asserts that by improving the quality, quantity, range, accessibility and cost of goods the consumer's quality of life will improve. As with the other marketing goals one can debate the merits of this one.

Maximising customer choice.

In terms of society, marketing touches us every day of our lives. We wake up to advertising (promotion) on the radio. When we read the paper over breakfast we encounter advertising. As we travel to work or school, we encounter advertising signs. In the shopping mall, we are bombarded with further advertising signs. When we collect our mail when we arrive home we encounter further advertising through junk mail and when we access the internet or watch television at night we again encounter advertising.

In fact we are subjected to so much advertising that we hardly notice that it is constantly before us.

One of the most blatant pieces of advertising that we encounter and even pay for is the advertising that we wear on our clothing in the form of "designer labels". Indeed all football clubs and many restaurants derive a great deal of their income from their merchandising departments.

Marketing, therefore, is designed to satisfy our needs and wants. Consumers' wants then become demands when they have purchasing power. These wants are satisfied by products already in existence or by products that are produced as a result of consumer demand or perceived consumer demand.

> **Focus Point**
>
> *The selling approach revolves around the idea of someone actively going out to sell a product.*

Quality of life is important to marketers.

Interdependence with other key business functions

As we saw in the Preliminary course the key business functions of a business involve operations, marketing, finance and human resources. Business cannot operate these functions in isolation. They need to be coordinated so that the business operates smoothly and productively.

How the key business functions of a business are coordinated often depends on business size. In a large business the key functions are usually separated into different departments or layers because these functions require different skills and knowledge. In this case staff are more specialised in their duties. It is here that the division of labour is apparent.

Key Business Functions

In a small business a manager or employee is usually required to carry out several tasks i.e. they have to be multi-skilled and they have to multi-task in the workplace. Usually this is not such a problem in a small business because the tasks don't require as high a level of skill. For example in a small business the manager may have to serve customers, answer the phone, accept deliveries, do deliveries and do basic accounting. This is not possible in a larger business.

As discussed in the section above, marketing is only one of the key business functions as can be seen in the diagram above.

Each business function relies on the other. Like a football team, there are specialist players in different positions who rely on the productive efforts of their team mates. If one player doesn't do what he or she is supposed to do then the whole team will fall down. For example, the Marketing Department requires information from the Accounting and Finance Department to see if there are sufficient funds available to undertake a particular marketing campaign and for them to actually fund the campaign. The Human Resources Department must supply the right personnel to staff the marketing project and the Operations Department must provide the correct resources to produce the product.

Interdependence occurs when each department recognises that they cannot work without each other and each is working towards common business goals. It is obvious that one department cannot work in isolation from another.

Production, selling and marketing approaches

Businesses will often use a variety of approaches in order to increase product awareness, satisfy the needs of customers and to increase profits.

Over the past 100 years there has been a number of marketing approaches used. The three main approaches to marketing have been:
- product approach
- selling approach
- marketing approach.

Marketing

Product approach (1900-1920)

The product approach revolves around the idea that if producers produced products and services, then consumers would want them. There was little or no consideration of the consumer and what they wanted. Businesses concentrated on producing as much as possible for as little as possible with no concern for customer preferences. They also concentrated on ways of increasing efficiency of production as a way of increasing sales and attracting customers. Businesses were **product** orientated. The production of the Model T Ford was a good example of this.

Efficient production enabled cars like the Model T Ford to be mass produced.

Selling approach (1930s-1960s)

The selling approach revolves around the idea of someone actively going out to sell a product. This approach developed after the Depression and during a period when goods were being produced faster than they could be sold i.e. supply was greater than demand. Businesses worked hard to attract customers so that supply and demand became more closely aligned.

Looking at it in another way Philip Kotler in his book *Marketing in Australia* describes the selling concept as that which "holds that the consumers will not buy enough of the organisation's products unless the organisation makes a substantial selling and promotional effort".

The selling approach and technique is a talent that has to be acquired if the more difficult products are to be sold. Products that are not foremost in the mind of consumers, such as life insurance and funeral plans have to be sold aggressively as the sales person tries to persuade the customer of the benefits of their product or service.

Focus point

The product approach revolves around the idea that if producers produced products and services, then consumers would want them.

Even products that are constantly in the mind of people have to be aggressively sold. A good example of this is the new and used motor vehicle industry where sales people have long ago perfected techniques to encourage the potential customer to buy the product.

There are as many selling techniques as there are categories of product or service- each one requiring a separate method of enticing the customer to make a purchase. Different media such as newspapers television, magazines and radio are used to convince the customer that they need the products.

The Marketing Concept (1960s - present time)

This concept looks at the fact that a business should identify a customer's needs and then service those needs. In this way the product will almost sell itself.

The **marketing concept** relates to the way a business achieves its goals by delivering its products and services more efficiently and effectively than its competitors. Products can be marketed on the basis of quality and value for money. This idea is based on the concept that if a product is of good quality, the consumer is likely to buy it.

The product can be marketed on the basis of consumer enticement i.e. where consumers wants and needs are determined first and then the business goes about satisfying those needs and wants. Mona Vale Education Centre on the northern beaches of Sydney established itself on this basis i.e. it was determined that there was a demand for quality tutoring services and the business set about satisfying those needs.

Here businesses must collect information on consumer trends in order to meet those trends. Marketers here began to focus on the 4Ps and develop a **customer orientation** and develop the concept of **relationship marketing.**

Customer orientation

What do we mean by a **customer orientation**? When identifying consumer needs the marketer must identify what the consumer wants and provide that product for them. Is it a new labour saving device, a new form of entertainment, a more functional motor car etc. When these wants are determined the business can set about satisfying these wants through production.

Even simply producing the product is not always good enough. The product must be good quality, user friendly and directly satisfy the consumers' needs, not approximately but directly.

It is here that market research is important in determining the wants of the public. Without carefully planned market research, the business may end up missing the target and develop a product that no-one wants. In that case all the promotion in the world will not make the product a success. For example, a number of years ago a white goods manufacturer developed a refrigerator with a microwave oven built in on top. It didn't sell and was withdrawn from the market. The reason it failed was not that consumers didn't want a refrigerator or a microwave but very few wanted both at the same time. This company obviously didn't do its market research thoroughly enough to determine what the customer wanted. It was not customer oriented.

Pricing is also of paramount importance. The customer must be able to afford the product or alternatively they must see that it is value for the money spent. For example a suit manufacture targeting the upper end of the market with a $2000 suit, while too expensive for some, must represent value for money for those who can afford it.

Service is important to the customer.

Distribution must be quick and efficient otherwise the customer will look to alternative products or to competitors to satisfy their needs and wants. In the 21st century, customers do not expect delays in the delivery of goods and services.

Promotion is made easier if the previous elements are in place, however the business still needs to promote its products skillfully if it is to penetrate the market successfully. This may involve selecting the right advertising agency, using the appropriate media and allocating the right amount of funds to the advertising budget.

Relationship marketing

Marketers must have a good relationship with their customers and this is where the term **relationship marketing** comes in. **Relationship marketing** is the developing of a personal relationship with customers as a way of marketing a product.

Customers demand a high level of service. Products such as soap, toothpaste or salt don't require a service to go with them, but a service is required with a more expensive product such as a motor vehicle and this service enhances the appeal of the product to the consumer. Also, an offer may consist of a major service with accompanying minor goods or services. For

> ### Focus Point
>
> *Relationship marketing is the developing of a personal relationship with customers as a way of marketing a product.*

example, airline passengers are buying a transport service—they arrive at their destination without anything tangible to show for their expenditure. However the trip may include some tangibles such as food and drinks.

An airline company, real estate agency or motor vehicle company must be aware of the relationship that should exist between themselves and their customers. Finally as part of this customer orientation and relationship marketing, businesses must use regular feedback from their customers to ensure that they are meeting all the needs of those customers and to ensure that they orient themselves towards customer satisfaction and in turn increased sales and greater profits.

A good example of this is the car dealership that sends movie invitations out to good customers or telephones after the vehicle has been serviced to see if the customer is happy with that service. Real estate agents often send

Focus Point

Customer orientation. When identifying consumer needs the marketer must identify what the consumer wants and providing that product for them.

Real Estate agents often send Christmas cards to former clients years after a sale has been made to keep up the relationship.

Christmas cards to previous clients in order to keep the relationship going.

Recently, manufacturers of goods have had to consider the attitude of society in their approaches to marketing. Increased environmental awareness has led to consumers demanding more environmentally friendly products in terms of emissions, wrapping and disposability. The need for this approach is not to be underestimated as we move through the 21st century.

Types of markets

There are many categories of markets found within the context of business operations. The following labels help to classify different market types:

- resource market
- industrial market
- intermediate market
- consumer market
- mass market
- niche market.

Resource markets

Focus Point

Resource markets are those markets for commodities such as minerals, agricultural products, people looking for work.

Resource markets exist for commodities (minerals or agricultural products), people looking for work (human resources) and financial resources. Resource markets are closely linked to industrial markets—see below. They may be local, larger domestic, or international markets. In resource markets, the producer doesn't see the eventual consumer.

Industrial markets

Industrial markets are concerned with the supply of goods and services to manufacturers and producers. They are not concerned with products for retail consumers. In this market business may be involved in many types of industry including manufacturing, construction, transport, communications, banking, finance, agriculture, forestry, fisheries, mining and public utilities. Businesses engaged in this market are often said to be engaged in "Business to Business" (B2B).

We can see from the diagram above that to make a pair of shoes, skins, chemicals, equipment, labour and energy need to be purchased on the industrial market to be further processed into the finished product.

Intermediate markets

These are reseller markets. These markets consist of businesses that acquire goods for the purpose of reselling them to others in order to make a profit. The main players in this market are wholesalers, retailers and importers. In the case of a wholesaler, they purchase goods from a manufacturer and sell them to a retailer. The retailer then sells them on to the consumer. Importers purchase goods from overseas and sell them domestically.

Wholesalers, retailers and importers act as purchasing agents for their own customers. These organisations purchase and resell most of the goods available, with the exception of the goods that are sold direct to the public by the manufacturer or grower.

Consumer markets

Consumer markets are the individuals and households who buy goods and services for personal consumption. Australian consumers spend over $250 billion each year in private consumption expenditure. It is usual to divide the consumer market into distinct demographic segments, such as

- the over 50s
- the under 25s
- young married couples without children
- young married couples with children
- the ethnic population
- the working woman etc.

In each case the marketer tries to anticipate what each consumer wants. Consumption decisions are strongly influenced by cultural, social, personal and psychological factors and the marketer must try to use these factors to their advantage.

Cultural factors are closely linked to one's social class. This is not such a strong aspect in Australia as it is in other parts of the world, but nevertheless does play a role in consumer behaviour and preferences.

Social factors include a person's reference groups i.e. groups having a direct or indirect influence on a consumer's behaviour, such as family, friends, neighbours, sports or entertainment idols. The last two have a great influence on the younger consumer.

Finally, psychological factors include the things that motivate consumers to purchase a product i.e. what needs they have to satisfy. Beliefs and attitudes also play a major psychological role in consumption behaviour. If a person believes that a particular type of car is better than an equivalent model by another maker they will often buy on emotional grounds rather than on factual information.

> **Focus Point**
>
> *Consumer markets consist of all the individuals and households who buy goods and services for personal consumption.*

How the different markets interact

The diagram below indicates the relationship between resource, industrial, intermediate and consumer markets. The manufacturer (who makes shoes) finds his raw materials, capital equipment and other inputs on the industrial market. He supplies his product (shoes) to wholesalers, importers or resellers (intermediate market). The goods are on-sold to retail stores who supply the end user (consumer market).

The Path from Raw Materials to Finished Goods

Inputs Sourced from the Industrial Market

Animal skins, Chemicals, Equipment, Labour, Energy

Manufacturer

Processes animal skins, using energy, labour, chemicals and equipment. Sells finished goods to wholesaler, and sometimes to retailer.

Wholesaler

Purchases shoes in wholesale (large) quantities, and resells them to individual retailers as required

Retailer

Displays shoes in store for consumers to purchase. The role of the retailer is to interpret the customers' requirements and supply according to perceived need. The role of the retailer is also to deal with any consumer complaint, and to negotiate with wholesalers and manufacturers on behalf of the consumer.

The retailer tries to anticipate what each consumer wants.

Mass markets are the markets that are aimed at consumers in a very broad sense because the products have universal appeal i.e. nearly everyone purchases these products. This is often called **market aggregation.** Products that fall into this category include gas, electricity and certain staple foods such as eggs, fruit and vegetables. This form of marketing doesn't require very specialised knowledge of the product and the marketing costs are often (but not always) a little lower than other forms of marketing.

The market for fruit and vegetables is an example of a mass market.

Niche markets are small, specialised markets catering for a small clientele. Here the business person has identified a small market that can be serviced profitably. The main thing that marketers look for here is establishing a competitive advantage in that market segment.

Surf tops is an example of a Niche market.

Businesses catering for niche markets are typically small retail outlets catering for such markets as clothing for the larger man or woman. Many small Australian filmmakers cater for a niche market as do some of the small boutique breweries.

REVISION EXERCISES 2.1

1. What does marketing consist of?

     _____

     _____

     _____

     _____

     _____

     _____

     _____

2. Briefly outline the **five** goals of marketing.

     1. _____

     2. _____

     3. _____

     4. _____

     5. _____

3. In business report format outline the ways in which marketing is interdependent with the other key functions of business. Remember to use dot point headings.

     _____

     _____

     _____

     _____

     _____

     _____

     _____

REVISION EXERCISES 2.1

4. List and define the **three** marketing approaches:

a. Explain what **customer orientation** and **relationship marketing** are and give examples of each.

_____

_____

_____

_____

_____

b. Using examples outline the **six** market types.

1 _____

2 _____

3 _____

4 _____

5 _____

6 _____

c. Select **one** of the following and draw up a list of industrial products that would go into that industry: manufacturing, construction, transport, communications, banking finance, agriculture, forestry, fisheries, mining and public utilities.

_____

_____

_____

_____

_____

2.2 Influences on Marketing

Factors influencing customer choice

What influences what we buy? The answer is not simple and encompasses several areas. For example, the type of toothpaste we buy may be a *psychological* decision. The type of restaurant we eat in may be a *sociocultural* one, the type of car we buy may be an *economic* one and *government* regulations affect the types of products we are allowed to buy.

Psychological Influences

Sometimes this is referred to as the behavioural basis for customer choice. Some businesses aim their marketing according to the behaviour they exhibit in the market place. A cosmetics or toothpaste company may wish to aim their marketing in this way.

Categories that can influence customer choice include:
- the number of times a product has been purchased
- the frequency of purchase
- loyalty to one brand of product
- identification with the product
- the perceived status of the product to the consumer
- the reasons for purchasing the product such as price, quality, durability or value for money.

From a **psychological** point of view, toothpaste advertisements may be driven by the concept of physical attraction or the killing of bacteria in the mouth which will give the consumer a better breath.

People often buy their tooth paste due to psychological reasons.

Sociocultural Influences

Marketers will group potential consumers according to **social, cultural** and **demographic** factors. Different people exhibit different customer choices depending on their position in the **sociocultural** spectrum.

Consumer choice is affected by:
- health issues
- lifestyle
- language
- religion
- nationality
- ethnic origins
- spoken language
- income
- social class
- age range and
- population distribution.

All consumers belong to multiple groups: their response to marketing will reflect the goals and aspirations of their social, cultural and demographic group membership. For example, a wealthy and educated Greek businessman living in the Eastern suburbs of Sydney may well exercise different consumer choices to a less well off Greek labourer living on the outskirts of the city. Religion will also influence consumer choice , particularly if the religion places taboos on certain types of consumption.

All of this indicates that the concept of **sociocultural** division is a very complex one. Since the end of World War II Australian attitudes and values have changed dramatically. With the arrival of migrants from Europe and later from Asia and the Middle East, Australians have become more cosmopolitan. This is reflected in the restaurants we eat in, the clothes we wear and the cars we drive.

In recent years consumer attitudes have changed towards products such as cigarettes, dairy foods and meat. On the one hand, there has been a shift towards healthy foods and the elimination of unhealthy consumption. On the other hand, our busy life style reflects the way we eat, fast food has become popular. The development of computer technology, the internet, social media and pay television has led people to access information in ways never known before. Society is now questioning basic and long held beliefs. Consumer values and attitudes are in a state of constant change.

Marketing strategies directed towards particular ethnic groups may well involve the medium and the message suitable to that group. For example some advertising signs on shops in Cabramatta (South Western Sydney) are in Vietnamese whilst those in Auburn are in Arabic. Some signs in Haymarket (Sydney) are in Chinese. There are Japanese signs on shops in Cairns (North Queensland).

Some radio stations and television channels have programs devoted to specific language groups. Advertising directed to Chinese speakers is programmed for times when the news and features programs are in Chinese, and so on for the other language groups.

Estimated Resident Population by country of birth			
2000		**2010**	
Australia	14,741,340	Australia	16,334,900
UK	1,126,880	UK	1,192,880
NZ	369,050	NZ	544,170
Italy	242,690	China	379,780
Vietnam	169,610	India	340,600
China	148,020	Italy	216,300
Greece	134,520	Vietnam	210,800
Germany	118,140	Phillipines	177,390
Phillipines	110,090	Malaysia	135,610
India	95,720	Germany	128,560

Source: ABS, *Migration, Australia* (Cat. No. 3412.0)

Marketers know that they must predict and/or adapt to this change quickly in order to capture the market. Marketers also know that each age group of people in the community buys different types of clothing, drinks, cars etc. This is not only because tastes change with age but because people do different things depending on which part of society they belong to. Good marketers predict trends for each age group or at least influence this trend once it has started - this is particularly true with the under 25 years age group.

Demographics

Closely related to **sociocultural** influences are **demographics.** The single most important demographic trend in Australia is the changing age structure of the population. The population of Australia is slowly getting older for two reasons. Firstly there is a slowdown in the birth rate and second, life expectancy is increasing. The diagram below indicates this is a worldwide phenomenon.

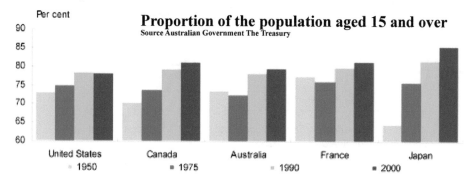

Per cent

Proportion of the population aged 15 and over

Source Australian Government The Treasury

United States   Canada   Australia   France   Japan

1950   1975   1990   2000

The changing age structure of the population will result in a different marketing strategy for the different age groups. This changing age structure of the Australian population will strongly affect future marketing decisions. Whereas in the 1950s & 60s the baby boomers were a bonanza for youth products (toys, education and leisure products) by the 21st century they often are the influential people in society, with money to spend on more luxury items. By 2015, when they reach the empty nest stage, their family commitments and mortgages should well have disappeared, and they will be more interested in financial services, travel, recreation and entertainment etc. By 2020 they will become Australia's senior citizens and they will present opportunities for retirement villages, medical services, home help and quieter recreational pursuits. Indeed the evolution of the "grey nomad" has seen a boom in sales of large recreational vehicles.

Other important demographic factors include the changing role of women who have entered the workforce in increasing numbers over the last thirty years, with many women now in a position of financial influence. This gives them a different form of spending power, creating a new and specialised market of their own.

The geographic distribution of the Australian population is also changing, with many southerners moving north to escape cold winters. Many of those moving north are retired couples. This is creating a larger "retired" market in the northern regions of Australia. However, the bulk of Australia's population (some 22 million), still lives along the eastern seaboard between Cairns and Geelong. Thus most of the marketing effort of business is directed towards urban dwelling coastal inhabitants.

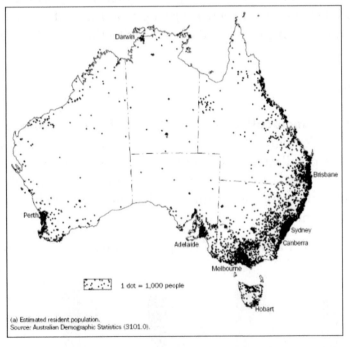

Australian population distribution - June 2006, 1301.0 - Year Book Australia, 2008, Australian Bureau of Statistics.

Economic Influences

This factor is a fairly broad one and can relate to the economic circumstances in which an individual finds themselves in, and it can relate to the state of the economy which in turn can affect customer demand. Obviously, the better off one is, the more choice they have with regard to the goods and services they can buy. The reverse is true for those not so well off.

In times of economic boom and full employment, consumer expenditure is high. These consumers are said to have purchasing power. This purchasing power is a function of people's income, product prices, domestic savings and the availability of credit. Marketers therefore, must be aware of trends in real income, savings and debt as well as changing consumer expenditure patterns in order to capture the best possible market share. The prevailing economic conditions at any one point in time can have a profound effect on the marketing strategy of a business.

Traditionally, the economy goes through four stages of the economic cycle: recession, expansion, boom and contraction. The marketing strategy employed by a business will depend on the stage of the economic cycle the economy is in at the time.

If a business is in an upswing or growth stage of an economic cycle, business marketers will try to predict the level of increased consumer demand that is likely to occur. Characteristically, during the upswing, demand increases to the point where it may outstrip supply, pushing prices up and forcing the Reserve Bank to increase interest rates in order to take the heat out of the economy. This increase in interest rates will reduce consumer demand in the short term. The marketer must try to predict these movements in the economy and the demand for their product that results. However, in general terms the marketer can take advantage of this increased demand by increasing the promotion of their products.

Recession results in low levels of economic activity, high levels of unemployment together with low levels of consumer demand. Promotion is a good strategy to increase demand at a time of falling demand, together with a reduction in prices to try to stimulate demand. Lower interest rates at this time (designed to stimulate economic activity) will help. It is at times like this that many businesses will offer interest free terms for up to six months for the purchase of goods - in the hope that attractive rates such as these will stimulate demand.

Government Influences

Customer choice and marketing decisions can be greatly affected by the political environment for several reasons. Legislation affecting business has increased steadily in recent years. This legislation has been enacted for several reasons. The first is to protect companies from each other. Business executives all praise the concept of competition but often try to neutralise it when it comes to them. For this reason legislation has been enacted to define and prevent unfair competition. These laws are enforced by the Australian Competition and Consumer Commission through the Competition and Consumer Act 2010.

The second purpose of government regulation is to protect consumers from unfair business practices such as misleading advertising, deceptive packaging and poor quality goods.

The third purpose of government legislation is to protect the larger interests of society against unfair business practices. For example businesses cannot produce products that will harm the environment or be unsafe for consumers. In other words the social costs of producing a product must be taken into account.

In this respect consumer choice is greatly affected by what can legally be sold to consumers such as the restrictions being placed on firearms, alcohol and tobacco products. Government regulations protecting consumers against false and misleading advertising influence consumer choice by eliminating bait advertising whereby a fictitious product is advertised at a very low price, the customer then being switched on to another, more expensive product once they are in the store.

Government regulations therefore influence customer choice in one way or another- usually by protecting the consumer even though it means restricting their choice.

Every business is influenced by government policy and regulations. Some laws are designed to regulate marketing specifically and others relate to the operation of business generally. Either way, these laws and regulations affect the way managers/marketers conduct their business.

In terms of government regulations, the Federal Government sets regulations to ensure fair trading between business. Section 92 of the Australian Constitution says that trade between the states must be free i.e. taxes cannot be charged. The Competition and Consumer Act (which is an Act specifically related to marketing) forbids price fixing between competitors as well as retail price maintenance. That is to say that competing businesses cannot get together to fix prices between themselves in order to remove competition and maintain market share. Likewise, manufacturers/suppliers cannot force retailers to charge a certain retail price. They can only recommend that retailers sell their product for a particular price.

Matters that are not the province of the Federal Government become State or Local Government responsibilities and may relate to such matters as anti-pollution laws, social justice legislation and health requirements.

The desirable level of government regulation is a matter for debate. Advocates of the free market philosophy would prefer to see less government regulation than more. They believe that unnecessary regulation adds economic costs, stifles business initiative and interferes with market mechanisms. The alternative view stresses the regulation of business as part of the government's responsibility to ensure sound economic and social management.

Consumer laws

Over the period 2010/11, consumer laws in Australia changed with the enacting of two new pieces of legislation:
- The Australian Consumer Law and
- The Competition and Consumer Act 2010.

From 1 January 2011, a new consumer law came into effect - the Australian Consumer Law. It provides Australia with one national law for fair trading and consumer protection. This law was achieved by the Council of Australian Governments in order to deliver a National set of regulations designed to reduce the complexity and duplication of the previous consumer laws for businesses and consumers.

The Australian Consumer Law (ACL) is a single, national consumer law and replaced the provisions in 20 national, State and Territory consumer laws.

According to The Hon David Bradbury MP (Parliamentary Secretary to the Treasurer) "Australian consumers and businesses will have the same rights and obligations wherever they are in Australia. In its Review of Australia's Consumer Policy Framework, the Productivity Commission estimated that a national approach to consumer law would deliver benefits of up to $4.5 billion per year". This would be achieved through the elimination of duplication and interpretation of the various state consumer laws.

According to the Australian Consumer Law website ACL includes:
- a new national unfair contract terms law covering standard form contracts
- a new national law guaranteeing consumer rights when buying goods and services, which replaces existing laws on conditions and warranties
- a new national product safety law and enforcement system
- a new national law for unsolicited consumer agreements, which replaces existing State and Territory laws on door-to-door sales and other direct marketing
- simple national rules for lay-by agreements
- new penalties, enforcement powers and consumer redress.

The ACL applies nationally and in all States and Territories, and to all Australian businesses. The ACL makes it easier for consumers to understand and enforce their rights because they will be the same across Australia.

The ACL is enforced and administered by the Australian Competition and Consumer Commission (ACCC), each State and Territory's consumer agency, and, in respect of financial services, the Australian Securities and Investments Commission (ASIC).

The ACL provides consumers with a law that is easy to understand. The ACL is simpler and clearer than the equivalent provisions of the Trade Practices Act and the State and Territory Fair Trading Acts. Complex legal terms have been replaced with terms that consumers can understand.

Consumers will benefit from better enforcement of the ACL:
- A single law will be uniformly enforced across Australia. A memorandum of understanding between regulators will ensure that this is the case.
- Courts and Tribunals across Australia will apply the same law to consumer disputes, allowing for cheaper and clearer avenues of redress.
- Uniform enforcement powers will be available to all consumer agencies across Australia.

Consumers benefit from clear rights under the ACL:
- Consumers will have the same rights under the ACL across Australia, no matter where they live, where they buy goods or services or where a supplier is located.

Businesses benefit from one law applying to consumer transactions across Australia:
- Businesses that trade in more than one State or Territory will only have to comply with one law.
- Regulatory complexity is often a deterrent for businesses when they consider expanding. The ACL will remove a barrier to interstate expansion of businesses.

The ACL provides businesses with a law that is easy to understand:
- Updated terminology, when compared to the archaic provisions in existing laws, can be more easily understood by businesses.
- A law that is easy to understand will result in fewer disputes, as businesses and consumers can have a common understanding of the ACL.

Businesses benefit from better enforcement of the ACL:
- Even when State and Territory laws are similar, differences in enforcement approaches can lead to additional compliance costs for businesses.
- Improved co-operation between consumer agencies applying the ACL will give businesses comfort that it will be applied consistently across Australia.

Business benefit from clear obligations under the ACL:
- The existing law imposes different obligations on businesses depending upon where in Australia a particular business, or a particular part of a business is located.
- The ACL will impose the same obligations on businesses across Australia, making compliance easier for businesses that trade in more than one jurisdiction.

The Australian Consumer Law in a Nutshell [PDF 593KB]

In 2010 the Competition and Consumer Act (2010) came into force. This replaced the Trade Practices Act 1974. While the new Act updates the Trade Practices Act, the general thrust of the new Act is similar to the old one.

One of the primary aims of the Act is to promote a level playing field for businesses of all sizes—including small and micro businesses—through fair competition. The Act does this by giving consumers and business rights that protect both parties in their dealings with suppliers, competitors and customers. It also imposes obligations on both parties in these dealings. Specifically the Act is designed to:

- Protect consumers against such things as false and misleading advertising and the misrepresentation of the contents of products
- Promote competition by stopping restrictive trade practices which stifles free enterprise

Deceptive and misleading advertising

Occurs when, in the promotion of a product or service, a representation is made to the public that is false or misleading. That representation may be through the promotion of the product that may be relating to product, price or place.

Laws have been enacted by governments to protect businesses from each other, to protect consumers from unfair business practices and to protect the community at large from unbridled business behaviour. The Australian Consumer Law underlines consumer law in Australia. Chapter 2 of the Act contains the main consumer protection provisions.

In terms of deceptive and misleading advertising, the Act prohibits misleading advertising, false claims about products or bait and switch advertising. This technique was widely used in the used motor vehicle industry before it was outlawed. Each of these items prevents marketers from taking advantage of consumers. If a product is advertised it must be exactly what it is advertised to be and do exactly what it is advertised it will do. Prizes and giveaways must be genuine with no hidden conditions. Bait advertising occurs when a non-existent item is advertised at a very low price in order to attract customers, only for them to be told the item has been sold but that they might like to consider another, similar item- at a higher price. This technique was widely used in the used motor vehicle industry before it was outlawed.

> **Focus Point**
>
> *Deceptive and misleading advertising occurs when, in the promotion of a product or service, a representation is made to the public that is false or misleading.*

Price discrimination

Price discrimination occurs when a seller charges different prices to different consumers for the same product. Doing this in itself is not unlawful, unless it is designed to freeze out the competition. The Act is not clear in this respect and any business or person who feels they were being discriminated against as far as price is concerned would have to prove this in court.

Implied conditions

Relates to the conditions of purchase whereby it is implied that the conditions of sale are realistic and reasonable. It sets out the main purpose of the promise made in a contract. If a manufacturer or retailer sells a good or service to a customer then it is implied that the good or service is of such a quality or will do the things required for the price being paid. For example, if a customer books into a five star hotel it is expected or implied that the room and room service would be of sufficient quality to justify the tariff being paid. If the room being delivered is of inferior quality then the customer would be entitled to a rebate on their tariff or if they wished , the customer would be entitled to cancel the contract and go and stay elsewhere.

Warranties

Are defined as both specific and implied conditions when products are sold which certify that the goods are fit for their purpose, are capable of doing the job, are of merchantable quality and meet the description. This also includes a set period where the goods are guaranteed to perform to contract and where the supplier will remedy any defect.

All products have a warranty. Even a small inexpensive item has an implied warranty that it will do the job it is designed to do. For example, a $20 toaster from a department store has an implied warranty that it will do the job for a reasonable amount of time. It is not compulsory for the customer to send off a warranty card to be able to claim warranty on the product. However, a receipt is important to show when the product was purchased.

Expensive items such as cars, televisions, refrigerators and computers etc will have a written warranty. If the product doesn't do what it is supposed to the customer is entitled to inform the manufacturer and have the problem fixed.

Unless expressly agreed otherwise, a breach of a warranty doesn't entitle the customer to cancel the contract, but they are entitled to sue for damages for non-compliance with warranty conditions. For example, the purchaser of a faulty motor vehicle can sue the car company if it refuses to fix items on the car that are covered by the warranty. (see opposite)

Here is an example of a Warranty provided by the manufacturer and the retailer when a cooling fan is supplied

MANUFACTURER'S WARRANTY

Do not operate any product with a damaged cord or plug, or after the product malfunctions, or is dropped or appears damaged in any way.

1. In addition to all rights and remedies to which you may be entitled under the Trade Practices Act 1974 (Cth) and any other relevant legislation, the manufacturer warrants this product to be free from defects in materials or workmanship for a period of 1 year from the date of purchase.

2. If you choose to make a claim under this manufacturer's warranty in relation to any such defects in materials or workmanship during the period of this warranty then we will, at our option, either repair or replace the product, or refund your money and take back the product. Our additional liability under the terms of this warranty does not extend beyond this, and we do not accept any additional liability under the terms of this warranty for consequential loss.

3. Our liability under this manufacturer's warranty is subject to us being satisfied that a defect was caused by defective workmanship or materials, and was not caused by or substantially contributed to by other factors, or circumstances beyond our control, including (but not limited to) defective installation, maintenance or repair, alteration or modification of the product in a manner not recommended by the manufacturers or any neglect, misuse or excessive use.

4. Please keep your sales docket, including cash register receipt, in a safe place as the docket will prove the commencement of the period of this warranty. If you wish to make a claim specifically under this manufacturer's warranty, you will be required to provide proof of purchase, preferably your sales docket.

5. The benefits conferred by this manufacturer's warranty are in addition to all rights and remedies conveyed by the Trade Practices Act 1974 (Cth), and any other statutory rights to which you may already be entitled, and this warranty does not exclude, restrict or modify any such rights or remedies that are implied by law.

Ethical aspects

Telling the truth

Truth in advertising has become an important aspect of ethical marketing in recent years. Deceptive and misleading advertising can have a negative impact on the acceptance of the product.

Not telling the truth when advertising a product can lead to legal action if the purchaser of the product suffers financial loss, physical harm or emotional stress. A product that doesn't do what it is supposed to do or is dangerous when used by certain people will make the business liable for damages.

Financial products that do not perform in the way the seller claims may result in financial loss or emotional stress for the consumer. Consumers can and do sue for loss due to false and misleading advertising.

Accuracy and good taste in advertising

As discussed above advertising must be accurate in its description of a product. Good taste in advertising is an important part of ethical advertising. There is what is known as the Australian Association of National Advertisers (AANA) Code of Ethics and this is monitored by the Advertising Standards Bureau.

Products that may damage health

In today's world of ethics, it is important to consider the marketing of products that may damage the health of the purchaser. In this case we are talking mainly of the legal products of tobacco and alcohol.

Let's look at tobacco first. Some people would argue that it is a legal product therefore it should be able to be advertised freely. However this argument comes mainly from the tobacco producers themselves. A number of years ago the advertising of tobacco was banned in Australia through television, bill boards, print media and sponsorship of sport.

In the end the slogan of "every cigarette is doing you damage" won through the argument with most people i.e. that there is no safe level of smoking as opposed to alcohol where a moderate consumption will not usually harm the consumer.

In recent years tobacco products have been placed out of site in shops and graphic health warnings placed on the packs. Indeed now the Federal Government has moved to ban any distinguishing packaging as a way of removing the identity of the product. This is because some people identified with a particular brand i.e. the psychological influence discussed in the section above. Indeed many tobacco companies promoted "lifestyle" images in their advertising. If you want to see some of these advertisements go to YouTube and take a look. Many of them are quite amusing when looked at in the context of what we know about the dangers of tobacco usage today. With the percentage of the population that smokes now down to around 18% and falling, it seems that the message is getting through.

However, the product is a legal one and the outright banning of the product would be an impossibility.

In terms of alcohol, it is generally regarded that there is a safe level of consumption. However, there is an ethical dilemma when it comes to the sponsorship of sport by alcohol companies. When we consider the problems of binge drinking and the over consumption of alcohol, then its consumption is damaging to health.

There have been many critics of sports such as Cricket, Rugby, Rugby League and AFL for having alcohol companies as major sponsors. There is then the association with the sport and drinking. This is especially relevant when we see footballers behaving badly after a night on alcohol when they should be role models for younger adults.

Away from sport it is important for alcohol companies to promote themselves responsibly and in most cases they do.

The promotion of fast food is another product that has come to the fore in terms of products doing harm to health. Again sporting teams, notably Cricket Australia has aligned itself with a fast food company by doing television endorsements, billboard advertising and logos on shirts. While no-one would claim that the consumption of fast food products occasionally will do any major harm, it is the regular consumption of this type of food that has contributed to the obesity epidemic that Australia is currently going through.

Another fast food company has long associated itself with junior sporting codes providing vouchers on a weekly basis for the "player of the day" etc. They have sponsored junior Tennis and many other events. In recent years due to negative publicity a range of "healthy choices" has been introduced into their outlets. However, the percentage of sales of these food products is very small.

Finally, in terms of products that can be damaging to health, it can be argued that the betting industry which is currently marketing via the various sporting codes can also be detrimental to health albeit in an indirect way. With the gambling industry entering the sponsorship of sporting teams which encourages gambling and the potential loss of money can affect the livelihood of families and therefore the family structure and therefore family health.

While each of the products discussed above are legal, the marketing of them needs to be done in an ethical fashion so as to not harm the health of those who consume those products. We can see that there is some government control over tobacco and alcohol advertising, it remains incumbent on the producers of those products to adhere to the appropriate code of conduct when marketing their products.

Engaging in fair competition

Sugging

Sugging (selling under the guise of research) is an off-shoot of telemarketing. Legitimate telemarketing is a tool used by a growing number of organisations to sell their goods and services to existing and potential customers by telephone. Specifically, telemarketing is the marketing of goods or services using the telephone as the principle medium of the customer or prospect. On the other hand sugging occurs when a marketer calls on the pretence that they are doing research, once they have found out information about the customer, they try to sell them a product based on that information.

From an ethical point of view the Australian Market and Social Research Society has a firm policy for telemarketing to follow so that sugging doesn't occur.

The AMSRS Policy on Telemarketing is as follows:

In outbound telemarketing or telephone interviewing, the respondent is to be made fully aware of the nature of the questions being asked and of the use to which the information being collected will be put at the beginning of the interview.

Where Telemarketing and Research are carried out by the same organisation, or group of organisations, the following steps should be taken, where practical:

    a. the name of the organisation carrying out the Research or Telemarketing activity must be clearly stated to the respondent at the beginning of the interview.

    b. respondents must in all cases be told the purpose of the call and the use to which the information asked of them will be put. This should occur as close as practicable to the beginning of the interview. For example, in the case of a research call, respondents may be assured that information provided by them will not result in a direct sales approach, and information provided by respondents will not be linked to them without their permission.

The AMSRS will take all feasible steps to ensure that the words "research", "survey" and "questionnaire" are not used by telemarketers when collecting information. The AMSRS discourages the use of the word "research" in the name of any company when engaged in telemarketing and encourages the use of a separate name for telemarketing activities.

All members of the AMSRS must abide by the MRSA Policy on Telemarketing, as part of the AMSRS Code of Professional Behaviour.

REVISION EXERCISES 2.2

1. List the **six** psychological categories that can influence customer choice.

   1 _____

   2 _____

   3 _____

   4 _____

   5 _____

   6 _____

2. Explain what is meant by the sociocultural factor influencing choice and give some examples.

   _____

   _____

   _____

3. Explain how economic factors can influence customer choice.

   _____

   _____

   _____

   _____

4. Outline some of the government regulations that can influence customer choice.

   _____

   _____

   _____

   _____

5. Explain the term "deceptive and misleading advertising" and give some examples.

   _____

   _____

   _____

   _____

REVISION EXERCISES 2.2 Page 2

6. Explain what is meant by "price discrimination"

_____

_____

7. What is a warranty and explain what warranties refer to?

_____

_____

_____

8. Why is it important to tell the truth when advertising?

_____

_____

_____

9. Outline products that may damage health.

_____

_____

_____

10. Outline why it is important for businesses to engage in fair competition.

_____

_____

_____

11. Explain the term sugging and describe what it relates to.

_____

_____

_____

2.3 The Marketing Process

Features of Marketing Plan

Developing a marketing plan usually involves
- Situation analysis (SWOT) and product life cycle
- Market research
- Establishing the market objectives
- Identifying the target markets
- Developing marketing strategies
- Implementing, monitoring and controlling:
  - including developing a financial forecast
  - comparing actual and planned results and
  - revising the marketing strategy.

Situation analysis: SWOT Analysis

This is where the business looks at, and analyses its strengths, weaknesses, opportunities and threats with regard to its position in the market place. By analysing its present position planners can determine a starting point for action. Next they analyse past, current and future trends in relation to their product, their company, market opportunities and their opposition. In other words the company must undertake a **situation analysis**. It is also appropriate to review the mission, goals and objectives of the business together with internal and external environmental forces affecting the business.

Effective planning involves constant re-evaluation of performance against the organisation's mission, goals and objectives. This process ensures that, with a changing business environment, goals are amended where necessary and the plan changes to meet emergent circumstances.

A useful technique to test the effectiveness of the planning process comparing performance to objectives is **gap analysis**. Here overruns or shortfalls are identified and corrective action is possible. For example, the level of sales may be lagging, and this may result in a shortfall of expected profits. If discovered early enough, advertising could be increased, or targeted, and the resultant activity could bring performance back in line with the plan.

Situation analysis should also include economic forecasts such as the likelihood of an increase in interest rates, a recession or increased competition from overseas. Economic factors can influence the business and its market, and must therefore be considered in any marketing plan.

Product Life Cycle

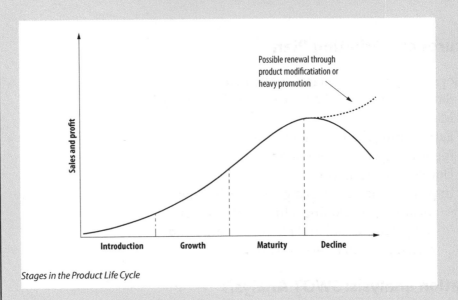

Stages in the Product Life Cycle

An important feature of a **situation analysis** is the **product life cycle.** The cycle varies for different products.

The **introductory** or **product launch stage** follows extensive market research, which establishes the need for the product. There may be heavy product development and promotional costs. These costs may exceed revenue from sales.

During the **growth stage**, the product begins to take off as sales begin to grow and brand loyalty is established. With increasing sales, the product begins to repay some of its establishment costs.

At **maturity**, the product has reached its peak of sales, is fully established in the market, and is contributing to profitability. However, competing products may have entered the market and market saturation may be near. Further growth may only be achieved by costly promotion.

Eventually, **decline** may result as consumer tastes change and new or alternative products emerge with better design or technical features. At this stage a decision has to be made whether to withdraw the product or extend its life through product adaptation, package change or promotion.

SWOT analysis will usually determine the effects of the product life cycle for inclusion in the marketing plan.

Market research

Market research involves:
- determining information needs
- data collection (primary and secondary)
- data analysis
- interpretation.

Focus Point

Research of the market is very important once the situation analysis has been carried out.

Market research is defined as the systematic collection and analysis of information and findings relating to a marketing situation faced by a company. In order to implement a marketing plan with confidence, the marketing manager must determine what information they need and collect **primary and secondary data** to support those needs and then analyse and interpret that data.

Determining Information Needs

Examples of the type of information that a marketing manager might need includes what competitors are producing, how they are producing it, what price they are going to charge, how they will package it and how it will be distributed.

Large businesses use marketing research personnel to gather information. Government departments, political parties and sporting organisations such as large football clubs also conduct market research. For example the AFL recently conducted major market research in western Sydney to determine the viability of the code in Sydney - a traditionally hostile, but growing market. They sent observers to football matches, conducted surveys in shopping centres, and interviewed prospective sponsors in the business community of Western Sydney.

GWS conducted market research before establishing an AFL team in Western Sydney.

In recent years market researchers have expanded their activities with the most common research activities involving business trends, long range forecasting, determining market characteristics, measuring market potentials, analysing sales, market share analysis, competitors, new product research, product testing, packaging research and research into the establishment of sales territories.

The trends in market research tend to be greater in consumer goods firms than in industrial goods firms because of the volatile nature of the consumer market compared to the industrial market.

A business may conduct its own research or it may outsource its research depending on the size of the company and the type of research being undertaken. In some cases smaller businesses receive research assistance from universities.

Data Collection

Data may be collected from primary or secondary sources. Primary sources may be:

- surveys
- discussion groups
- observation
- experimentation.

Sometimes all of the research objectives can be achieved by using secondary research data i.e. data that is already in existence and usually collected by someone else for some other purpose.

Primary research

Surveys

Surveys may be conducted by mail, over the telephone (one of the most common methods), or in person in the home or in the street. The response from surveys sent through the mail is poor due to the effort required from the respondent—even when the postage has already been paid. A one-to-one contact between the market research analyst and the respondent usually produces a positive response to a questionnaire.

In structured surveys every respondent is asked the same question from a formal list.

Unstructured surveys have a more open format and allow the interviewer to ask further questions according to the respondent's answers.

Surveys are an excellent way of collecting information

Within the structured and unstructured surveys, research may be direct or indirect. In the indirect approach the researcher asks direct questions such as "why didn't you like the game today?" Indirect questions might be "What sort of people do you think attend these games?" Survey research is the most commonly used method of collecting primary data and indeed is often the only method used in a research project.

Discussion groups

These are usually carried out in the home or other convenient location. Comfortable surroundings encourage open responses. The results are sometimes biased as an individual's response may be influenced by other people's responses. Respondents may agree more easily than oppose the ideas of another within a group.

Observation

Gathering data by observing people's behavior is also a legitimate form of market research. For example a football club may hire a research company to discover what patrons felt about a game and the quality of service and comfort they experienced. They may observe patrons' level of seating comfort during a game, ease of obtaining refreshments, enjoyment of pre-match entertainment, ease of transport to the ground or the apparent reactions to the entertainment provided by the game.

Observation can be carried out directly by being present at the game, or in simulated situations. Observation has even been carried out using one-way mirrors or hidden cameras. However the market researcher has to be careful here as there are privacy and ethical issues involved if the participant doesn't know they are being observed.

Experimental research

When introducing a new product or additive to a product, it may be possible to obtain information by experiment. For example respondents may be given a sample of the new product being introduced together with samples of other products for comparison. They might also use a number of questions to go along with the experiment such as "Which product/additive did you prefer?" "How often would you use it?"

> **Focus Point**
>
> *Secondary research is data that is already in existence and usually collected by someone else for some other purpose.*

Whether it is surveys, discussion groups, observation or experiment, marketers must know who they are going to sample. For example there is no point in sampling people living in inner Sydney about a particular type or brand of tractor or cane harvester. Therefore part of the plan for collecting information must involve a knowledge of:

- **Sample population**: those who are likely to be interested in purchasing the product or service.
- **Sample size:** How many people should be sampled. Large samples are more reliable than small ones. However, small samples can be very reliable providing the sampling procedure is thorough. For example, the small sample should be representative of the whole potential market, not just for those from a particular geographic or socio-economic area.
- **Sampling frame:** This refers to the fact that each member of the potential market has an equal chance of being selected in the sample. For example, if a telephone company wishes to survey its customers, it should have a data base of those customers and be able to select them at random to respond to the survey.
- **Sampling procedure:** Sampling procedure must be as thorough as possible. Random sampling requires that each person has an equal chance of being selected. Random telephone numbers or post code selection can be used.

Secondary research

Secondary research data is very useful for the marketer who can use information such as demographic information (age make-up, ethnic make-up, sex and marital distribution, socio- economic distribution, distribution of religious groupings etc). This data can be accessed quickly, easily and cheaply to help the marketer to locate potential markets and help them decide where to concentrate their promotional activities and the type of promotion that they will employ.

This **secondary research** may even determine which elements of the **marketing mix** to concentrate on i.e. product, price, promotion, place. Secondary research data can be found using the following sources:

- Internal records of their own business by checking such data as customer enquiries, customer details and statistics (such as previous use of the product). From this information they may be able to develop a customer profile which they may not already have. They may be even able to make projections about future use of the product by their customers based on previous sales, such as seasonal usage.
- Government web sites e.g. the Australian Bureau of Statistics (ABS) which are one of the major sources of data in Australia. All government departments publish journals of research together with general statistical information. This information is very valuable, particularly in relation to potential and target markets as well as demographics.
- Trade and professional associations such as the various Chambers of Commerce, Employers Federation, Australian Chamber of Manufactures, The Business Council of Australia and The Small Business Association all produce statistical research and journals which can provide the marketer with valuable customer information.
- Other marketing firms who have carried out their own primary and secondary research specializing in areas that are of interest to the current researchers.
- Universities research organizations and foundations who carry out social research through their own research departments and publications. Indeed, these organizations often welcome other organizations using their work. This information, being for general use is known as "public domain" information.
- Other published sources such as trade magazines and newspapers and the internet generally.
- Data Miners. These are organisations which use huge data bases to pinpoint consumer preferences.

Data Analysis

Interpretation

The next stage is the implementation of the research plan. All of the information developed earlier has to be collected, collated and analysed. This is the most expensive stage and most subject to error. It is expensive because it is time consuming and may require expensive information technology to process. It is subject to error because detailed analysis must take place to interpret the data. Care must be taken because if any of the data is misinterpreted the whole campaign could come to very little.

The researcher must now interpret the findings, draw conclusions about the implications, and report them to management. Interpretation is then carried out by management who is familiar with the objectives of the research. Management must also check and ultimately be responsible for the accuracy of the findings. In addition it is management who must ultimately decide what action to take once the research findings are reported and agreed upon.

This interpretation is important because, as with the previous phase, incorrect interpretation will make the whole research process useless. It should also be pointed out that a large amount of effort has been expended up to this point, well before any product has been developed or marketing strategy applied. However, it is very important that the groundwork is completed. It may save a lot of resources later and lead to significant success in sales.

Establishing market objectives

Once the business has established its mission, goals and broad objectives, it must now look to specific market objectives.

- **Increasing market share.** This may be achieved by:
  - reducing prices to make the product more competitive
  - improving quality of the product
  - establishing, better and more efficient distribution.
  - improving the efficiency and productivity of sales staff
  - using incentive bonuses for sales staff
  - increasing market expenditure (i.e. increasing advertising).
- **Extending product range.** New products emerge through:
  - **research and development** (Research and development will provide the company with the technical know-how to be able to add a new product to their range)
  - **market research**. (Market research will help determine which new products should be manufactured-and placed on the market.)
  - **new technologies** (The growth of personal computing devices with increased miniaturisation and accelerating processing speeds has created new opportunities in every market.)

An increasing product range can create new markets for the business that were previously untapped. For example, most sports shoe companies market a range of running shoes from low priced, low tech models (used largely as walking shoes) to high priced, high tech models (used by keen runners). There are often models in between, that cater for runners who roll outwards when they run, models for those who roll in and therefore require ankle support and for those who have heel problems when they run.

- **Expand geographically** A business may expand its market by selling its product in other cities or interstate. The business may increase its level of activity by:
  - establishing branch offices
  - developing franchise partnerships
  - appointing agency representation
  - setting up remote distribution networks. As a business grows and expands its distribution networks sales and revenues will increase.
  - expanding the sales force located in regional areas.
- **Expand through export:** A business may commence international marketing because:
  - weak marketing opportunities at home
  - the tax burden may be too heavy at home
  - the government might provide export incentives global marketers can take advantage of economies of scale. Larger companies have lower unit operating costs and therefore higher profitablility
  - export marketing helps to cushion economic cycles
  - information and technology available overseas may be adopted by the business.
  - other countries sometimes have more favourable cost structures

▪ **Maximise customer service.** Maximising customer service is one of the most important functions of marketing in the 21ˢᵗ Century. Customers, are an important business asset: neglecting customers will allow competitors to steal market share. So much increased business is a result of customers feeling happy with the way they have been treated and this occurs in three ways:
   - satisfaction with the product
   - satisfaction with the way sales staff interact with the customer
   - satisfaction with the after sales service

▪ **Greater market penetration.** Managers must work out a way to attract more customers away from other brands while not losing present customers. To do this a company might
   – cut the price of its product
   – increase the advertising budget
   – improve the advertising message, or
   – get into more stores and improve shelf position in those stores.

▪ **Obtain Price advantage.** A lower priced product is more likely to be in higher demand. Economists talk about price elasticity of demand, where small decreases in price result in increased sales. Increases in price result in reduced sales. A small decrease in price will see demand increase greatly. In this case price competition is very strong. Petrol falls into this category. For example if a service station puts up its price by 1 cent a litre customers will go to an opposition service station if that service station is close by. If demand is inelastic, a small increase or decrease in price will see the demand for the product relatively unchanged, meaning that competition for sales rests with product differentiation rather than price.

> ## Marketing Objectives
>
> - Increase market share
> - Extend product range
> - Expand geographically
> - Expand through export
> - Maximise customer service
> - Obtain greater market penetration
> - Obtain price advantage

Identifying target markets

When selling an existing product or developing a new one, the business needs to know where and how it will be sold, i.e. what is their target market. By definition a target market is a section of the public to whom the producer aims his/her products and marketing campaigns.

Possible target markets are:

- the youth market
- young married couples
- singles
- mature age
- the elderly
- he lower end of the price range
- the top of the range
- a combination of the above.

Markets may divided broadly into four segments:

- mass markets (the broad market)
- concentrated markets (small market areas where specialist products are provided)
- differentiated markets (where producers provide consumer choice by product differentiation as in the motorcar market)
- niche markets.

Choosing a **target market e**nables a business to focus its marketing program on those consumers most likely to respond.

Forecasting

The **potential market** is the set of consumers who have some level of interest in a product. Potential consumers must have enough income to afford the product. Therefore the size of the market is often a function of income. Access barriers further reduce the market size. If a product is not distributed in a particular area for whatever reason, potential customers are lost to marketers.

The **penetrated market** is the set of consumers who have already bought the product. Depending on the product, these consumers may be unlikely to purchase the product again.

Forecasting future demand is the art of anticipating what buyers are likely to do in the future. Forecasting the size and growth of any market is difficult. It is particularly difficult when we attempt to forecast the size of a new market. (e.g. electronic equipment and other technological products- consumers have no experience in using the products.) The forecaster must consider possible reactions to the product by consumers and competitors There are several ways to do this:

- survey the potential market
- ask your sales staff
- seek expert opinion from dealers, distributors, suppliers, marketing consultants

■ analyse past sales. Many firms prepare their forecasts on the basis of this.

■ leading indicators. Many firms try to forecast sales by finding out how the demand for other products is going. For example, a hardware firm may base some of its sales forecasts on figures relation to such things as the number of building approvals and houses that have been commenced in the previous months.

Primary and Secondary Markets

Many marketers divide their target market into **primary target market** and the **secondary target market.** The primary target market is the main group of people to whom the product is aimed: the main thrust of any marketing campaign is directed towards the primary target market.

A secondary target market is a smaller group who also buy the product. The secondary market should not be ignored as it will produce extra sales and add to profitability.

This point is illustrated by the following example. The Ford motor company markets a table top utility truck with special suspension and high tech air cleaning systems for country roads. Its primary target market is the farmers and rural dwellers. Its secondary target market is city dwellers.

Developing marketing strategies

Marketing strategies enable a business to access the target market meeting its goals effectively. The 4P's, Product, Price , Promotion and Place are a feature of this process. In the context of marketing:

■ **Product:** includes all the different goods and services that are offered to customers, the way they are packaged and the types of after sales service offered. Careful product design gives satisfaction to the customer by meeting their needs effectively.

■ **Price:** the cost to the consumer of the product in the market place. Included here are the methods of pricing used, as well as discounts and credit terms. This is something that the marketer must consider very carefully. Price levels affect the demand for the product. High prices will result in slow sales. Low prices will increase sales but will reduce profitability. Break even may be too difficult to achieve. Price must be in line with value or consumers will purchase the competitors products.

■ **Promotion:** Advertising, publicity or sales promotions are included here. How a product or service is presented to a customer will depend on the target market of the business, the size of the business and the type of product being sold. Determining an efficient promotional strategy often requires a lot of analysis and careful planning.

■ **Place: This refers** to distribution, storage and delivery that are used for the product. Large capital items are often produced to order, and delivered to the end user from point of manufacture. Smaller items may be manufactured in bulk, and distributed to multiple retail sites for sale to end users. A **Place** strategy will be tailored for specific products.

Using the marketing plan

Implementation

A key element of an appropriate marketing strategy will result in having the right *product* on the market. It involves employing the right *promotional* methods, using the right pricing techniques and distributing the product in the right place.

Part of this process is the development of a detailed action program to ensure tasks are well understood, that they are carried out on time, and the management decisions are put into practice.

An effective organisation structure with the right mix of human resource and management is necessary for success. Good communications systems will ensure the procedures are understood and followed. Failure to implement the marketing plan properly may result in poor sales, profit levels and even product failure.

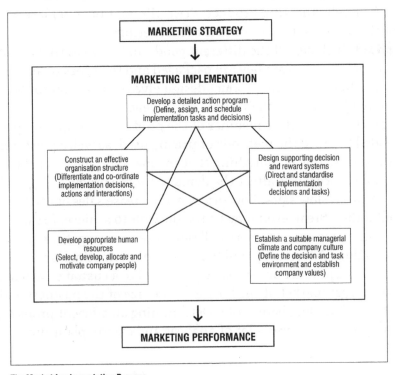

The Market Implementation Process
Source: *Marketing in Australia*, Kotler *et al*, p.639

The Market Implementation Process

Monitoring

There is little purpose in devising and implementing a marketing plan if there is no evaluation of the success or otherwise of the whole operation. If necessary the whole marketing strategy may need to be revised if the results are not what was anticipated.

What is required here is a recording and reporting of actual and expected results when a plan is implemented. Management information systems should compare:
- financial forecasts and results
- sales forecasts and results
- market projections and actual statistics
- market share projections and performance
- profitablity and sensitivity analysis.

There are two basic marketing costs:
- **Order-getting** costs such as research, selling, advertising, promotion, warranties and packaging.
- **Order-filling** costs such as shipping, warehousing, inventory control staffing and order processing.

Management reports-Monitoring

- **Sales and Market:** It is here that the marketer measures actual sales against projected sales in terms of quantity and revenue. This type of analysis doesn't just look at the total sales of the business but also breaks it down into its parts. For example, it will look at each product line, where they are being sold (territories), changes in volume of sales, target markets and sales figures of individual sales representatives. The need to break sales figures down into parts is important. Which product lines are doing best and why? In what areas are they selling best? Is the product selling to the expected target market or to a market sector that is unexpected?
All of these factors have to be taken into account when monitoring the marketing plan. The results of the findings must be acted on to counter any down turns in demand in any area.
- **Market share analysis:** This analysis involves comparing market share with ones competitors. If market share has declined, then answers have to be found as to why. There can be any number of reasons such as improved standards and innovation from competitors, changed consumer tastes, intensified price competition, distribution problems, greater effort on the part of sales representatives or new advertising campaigns.
Whatever the reason for a decline in market share, the business must address the problem when it is identified. Even if this analysis discovers that the market share has increased, the reasons must be established so that the company can work to increase any strengths it might have.

- **Profitability by product/territory:** Because most medium and large businesses market more than one product, it is important to look at the profitability of each product being marketed and not just the overall profit. This is because one product line that is performing poorly will bring average company profits down. It does not make good business sense to have several strongly performing products supporting one weak one. In this case the business must seriously consider eliminating the poorly performing product. Alternatively, a renewal strategy will need to be employed in order to lift the sales of the ailing product.

  The same goes for the monitoring of particular territories. If one territory is not reaching its sales targets, the company must know why. It may need to put a new sales strategy into the area or perhaps even withdraw from that territory altogether—depending on the reasons for the poor performance in that territory.

  When the business has established where its strengths, weaknesses, opportunities and threats lie in terms of its marketing plan, several issues need to be considered. Once the business has monitored the marketing plan, it must revise its marketing strategy if needed. It can do this through:

- **Change in the marketing mix:** Depending on the results of the monitoring, the business may need to change one or more of four elements of the marketing mix i.e. *product* (packaging, positioning, warranties etc) place (discounts, credit terms, payment period etc) *promotion* (advertising, sales promotion etc) place (location of markets, warehousing, distribution, transport and inventory). Remember there is no correct mix. It will depend on the individual firms circumstances as to the emphasis it places on each of the 4Ps.

- **New product development:** All businesses should always be on the look out for new product ideas. Modifications to the marketing plan may specifically involve this, particularly if the product has reached the maturity or decline stage in its life cycle.

- **Product deletion:** Once a product has run its course and sales and profits have declined the company may decide to delete that product altogether. This may be a result of technological advances, shifts in consumer tastes or increased domestic or foreign competition. A company cannot afford to carry a weak product because it can be very costly.

  Unproductive resources have to be put towards the business in order to prop it up in the form of product promotion. The most economical thing for the business to do is eliminate the product altogether if it cannot be renewed.

- **Allocation of human resources:** Often a marketing plan review exposes weaknesses in the way human resources have been allocated to marketing tasks. This may involve development staff, sales staff, advertising staff, accounting staff etc. Training and development may be needed to bring all staff up to scratch. The company may need to spend some time on refocusing on its mission statement and clarify its aims and objectives.

Controlling

Once each of these costs have been estimated, the business manager will compare them with the potential benefits of that expenditure and a decision will be made as to the degree to which they will be implemented i.e. the **cost benefit analysis** is undertaken. Essential here is an analysis of the **projected costs and revenues,** if the marketing plan is to continue to operate without a change in direction.

Revenues may also need to be broken down by **market territories, company division and representatives.** If the monitoring identifies poor performance corrective action may be necessary. Alternatively if performance beyond expectation is identified, then the efforts should be regarded. The task of management is to manage. Planning and monitoring are the tools of management enabling managers to control, and provide leadership whilst change is undertaken

Business constantly experiences change. New competitors enter the market with new products, old ones leave. Consumer tastes change and so do the demographics of the market place. Constant monitoring of the marketing plan will track change in the market place. If the marketing plan is monitored and evaluated in relation to external factors (such as competitors) and internal factors (such as finances) then the marketer can adjust their plan accordingly.

Interactive Planning

Planning, implementing, monitoring and controlling are not independent functions: they do not occur in isolation. Monitoring an implemented plan will always highlight gaps between what is expected and what is observed.

Management action will follow and new directions will be established. There will be of necessity a new or modified plan. New strategies will be formulated and new targets, and performance will result.

The cycle continues, and the business undergoes change, some generated by external stimuli, and some produced by change from within.

REVISION EXERCISES 2.3

1. Define the term situation analysis.

_____

_____

_____

_____

2. What is a SWOT analysis?

_____

_____

_____

_____

_____

_____

_____

_____

_____

3. Draw the product life cycle diagram and explain its operation.

_____

_____

_____

_____

_____

_____

4. Complete the table below by giving examples of each type of research.

PRIMARY	SECONDARY

5. List the seven marketing objectives and briefly explain each.

1 _____

_____

_____

2 _____

_____

_____

3 _____

_____

_____

4 _____

_____

_____

5 _____

_____

_____

6 _____

_____

_____

7 _____

_____

_____

6. Explain the concept of target market.

_____

_____

_____

7. List the **four** marketing strategies and briefly describe each.

1 _____

2 _____

3 _____

4 _____

8. Make brief notes on:

a. market plan implementation

_____

_____

_____

b. monitoring and controlling

_____

_____

c. developing a financial forecast

_____

_____

_____

d. comparing actual and planned results

_____

_____

_____

e. revising the marketing strategy

_____

_____

_____

2.4 Marketing Strategies

Market segmentation

(This section will look at the 4Ps of marketing in addition to the market segmentation and product/service differentiation below)

There are several ways of segmenting markets and differentiating products as we will see. A segment is a part of a market. In many ways just like the segment of a mandarin. It allows the identification of portions of the market that are different from one another.

Marketers must understand customers' needs. The drawback of mass marketing is that customer needs and preferences differ and the same offering is unlikely to be viewed as optimal by all customers. If firms ignore the differing customer needs, another firm is likely to enter the market with a product that will serve that specific group.

Target marketing divides the market up into segments in order to service the customers' specific needs. For segments to be useful they should be:
- Identifiable: They should be able to be identified
- Accessible: The segments should be able to be reached through advertising media
- Substantial: The segments should be sufficiently large to justify spending marketing dollars on them
- Unique: They must be different to other segments of the market
- Durable: The segments should not be constantly changing so that there is minimal costs of frequent changes.

Markets can be segmented according to the following characteristics:
- Geographic/physical
- Demographic
- Psychographic
- Behavioural

Geographic Physical Segmentation

The following are the ways a market can be segmented geographically.
- **Region/location:** This refers to the place of selling or marketing of the product. Areas of location might be the metropolitan area, a large regional centre such as Tamworth or a small rural town. A good case in point is the selling of sugar cane harvesters to cane farmers in towns along the Queensland coast between Nambour and Cairns. In this case the target market is very much a location based one. Likewise

manufacturers of sheep shearing clippers will target farmers in the wool growing industry right across Australia

- **Size:** How big is the market for a given product? The market size for the local butcher shop is small, catering for only local and regular customers. Promotion is usually through the local newspaper or by flyer advertising the weekly specials. Medium to large businesses selling their products within one city or region of a city may choose local print media, billboards, radio or television to promote their products.

- At the other end of the scale is the large public company whose physical market area is the whole of Australia or even the entire globe. Product promotion is expensive and often handled on a regional basis. For example, advertising of Coca Cola or Ford in Australia is handled through the local advertising budget.

- **Share:** Market share refers to the percentage of sales that a product has. Market share is something jealously guarded by producers, knowing that it is only temporary and subject to competition from other businesses.

- **Location:** This refers to the place of selling or marketing of the product. Areas of location might be the metropolitan area, a large regional centre such as Tamworth or a small rural town. Here promotion will depend on the location of the produces and subsequent target market. A good case in point is the selling of sugar cane harvesters to cane farmers in towns along the Queensland coast between Nambour and Cairns. In this case the target market is very much a location based one.

- **Industry:** Segmentation in this situation relates to specific industries. As in the example above producers may target sugar cane farmers with their harvesters. Likewise manufacturers of sheep shearing clippers will target farmers in the wool growing industry right across Australia

- **Population distribution:** These are usually classified as urban, suburban, or rural. Each of these market segments has different customer needs. For example, the rural dweller is likely to buy a different type of motor vehicle to their city cousin. People living in areas close to the city often have different needs to say families living in the suburbs.

- **Climate:** People living in different climate areas of Australia have differing needs in terms of clothing, food, housing etc and this in itself creates a geographic market segment.

Markets can be segmented by location and industry.

Demographic Segmentation

Demographic features include age, gender, income, family size, education etc. Obviously, marketers of products will aim their marketing strategy towards the appropriate target market.

One important point to make here is that with each of these demographic segments many people will fall into more than one category and therefore find themselves the target of many different promotions.

One demographic category is 'Family'.

Some demographic segmentation categories include:

- **Age:** People of different ages have different needs in terms of housing, motor vehicles and life-style.
- **Gender:** The difference between the purchasing choices of men and women.
- **Family size:** Single person households up to large families have different purchasing requirements. The requirements of a single person household are often fairly simple. We all know someone who lives on their own. A large family of say 10 people has transport problems, different clothing and housing needs and are often (but not always) in the lower socio-economic brackets.
- **Family life cycle:** As family structure changes from the full nest household of say 5 to the empty nest stage (when all the children have left home) the housing requirements, motor vehicle requirements and clothing requirements change. Sometimes the parents down size their home at this time. They no longer need a people mover as their car etc.
- **Generation:** baby-boomers, Generation X etc. Baby-boomers were born between 1947 and about 1960 and are now in the older age brackets and have different purchasing requirements to Generation X people. They differ in clothing, music, entertainment, restaurants etc. Baby-boomers also are often financially comfortable, having paid their house off etc.

- **Income:** This is an obvious one. The greater the income level, the greater the spending power. Wealthier people will be targeted in terms of cars and other "life-style" products and services.
- **Occupation:** We all know the occupations where people make more money and those that don't so it is obvious which occupations will be targeted for the more expensive items as in the point above.
- **Education:** This is often (but not always) linked in with the two points above and so doesn't require repetition.
- **Ethnicity:** This is an interesting one in terms of food and clothing in particular
- **Nationality:** Similar to the point above.
- **Religion:** This is not a strong element because people of different religious beliefs come from a range of socio-economic backgrounds. In terms of religious purchases, it is a relatively small market.

These are the broad demographic segments. Indeed if we want to be even more definitive we can see that many of these variables have categories within categories. For example, family life cycle can be expressed as bachelor, married with no children (DINKS- Double Income, No Kids), full-nest, empty-nest or solitary survivor. Some of these categories have several stages. For example, full-nest 1, 2, 3 depending on the age of the children. However we don't need to concern ourselves in this course with this level of detail.

Psychographic Segmentation

Psychographic segmentation groups customers according to their lifestyle, activities, interests and opinions. Some psychographic variables include:

- **Activities:** People who participate in sport (cycling, tennis, football and cricket etc) are a segment that is targeted by sporting equipment and apparel manufacturers.
- **Interests:** These can include hobbies, sport (again), leisure activities such as the theatre, art galleries etc all of which will attract marketers selling say subscriptions to the theatre etc.
- **Attitudes:** People have attitudes towards things such as sport, gambling and alcohol which can influence their purchasing decisions.
- **Values:** These values may influence the clothing that they wear and (as above) their attitudes towards gambling and alcohol which can influence their purchasing decisions.

Behavioural Segmentation

The behavioural basis for segmentation is based on actual behaviour towards products. Some businesses segment their market according to the behaviour they exhibit in the market place. A cosmetics or tooth paste company may wish to segment their market in this way. Categories include:

- Frequency of purchase. The more often a person purchases a product such as certain types of grocery items.

- Loyalty to the one product. Some people remain loyal to one particular product because they have always purchased that product or listened to a particular radio station- simply out of loyalty.
- Perceived status of the product to the consumer. Some people will purchase a product (such as a motor car) because of the status they think it gives them. They like to be seen in that type of motor vehicle.
- Reasons for purchasing the product (price, quality, durability, value for money). On a behavioural basis, some people will purchase a particular product because they are not "prepared" to pay a higher price for a certain product if they think they are being "ripped off". Others will purchase a product only if it is of a certain quality or durability and therefore of a certain value for money.

The concept of market segmentation can be rather confusing because different texts have a slightly different take on what a makes a "market segment". The most important thing to remember is that a market segment is a part of a market that a business is aiming their products and services at.

Product/service differentiation and positioning

Product differentiation can be defined as "the variation between a number of models of the same basic product e.g. a brand of washing machine with six available models". An important aspect of marketing strategies is to be able to differentiate ones product from another firms product. It is also designed to provide a point of differentiation within their own product range. Many businesses will differentiate their product from their competitors by having several different models of the same thing.

> **Focus Point**
>
> *Product differentiation is the variation between a number of models of the same basic product.*

Product/service differentiation is somewhat different to market segmentation. Here the seller produces two or more products that exhibit different features, styles, quality and so on. For example, (as discussed above) Coca-Cola produces several soft drinks packaged in different sizes and containers. They are designed to offer a variety to buyers rather than appeal to different market segments. In this way Coca-Cola can also maximise its share of the soft drink market by effectively squeezing out the competition and competing against itself.

In the case of a car company they may develop different models, different styles and designs, provide fast and reliable service and longer warranty periods than their competitors in order to out-do their competitors.

In terms of service differentiation the same principle holds true. A law firm may offer a range of legal services or a dental practice may offer a range of dental procedures from normal dentistry through to cosmetic dentistry that other dentists don't offer.

Product positioning is a key aspect of the marketing mix. It's the image a product has in the mind of a consumer. Products can be positioned in the market according to price and quality, image, target market or its competition. For example "No Frills" brand of grocery lines are positioned at the lower end of the market, some cars are positioned according to image and target market while various brands of jeans are positioned at various ends of the market.

It is at this point that we will look at the 4Ps of product, price, promotion and place in more detail as marketing strategies.

Product	Place
Features	Channels of distribution
Options	Inventory
Style	Locations
Brand name	
Packaging	
Sizes	
Service	
Warranties	
Returns policy	
Positioning	

Price	Promotion
List price	Advertising
Discounts	Personal selling
Allowances	Sales promotion
Payment period	Publicity
Credit terms	

The product is the good or service that is offered for sale. The product is designed to give satisfaction to the customer. As the diagram above shows, ideally a product will have the following characteristics:

Brand name

Every product must have a brand name that is well known trusted and recognisable. A brand name such as this reinforces the product in the mind of the consumer. The brand name will promote the product to the consumer. If we think of any of the well known brand names such as Nike, Apple, Sanyo, Ford, Levis etc (the list is endless), we immediately have a product in mind as well as the quality of that product. This is where the logo is so important. The Nike "swoosh" tells it all.

Packaging

Product packaged attractively and well will sell much more readily than one that is not. Customers shop with their eyes much the same as we recognise a good meal by what it looks like just as much as the way it smells and tastes. Therefore good marketers know that they have to package their product attractively. We only have to look on supermarket shelves to see the role that packaging plays regarding product.

However in today's market place, consumers are demanding that packaging be environmentally friendly and provide information about the product where possible. For example, Sanitarium Weet-Bix is attractively packaged and at the same time has nutritional information on the side panels of the packaging.

Brand name and packaging are not the only aspects of product. There are a number of others that the student should be aware of and these include:

- **quality:** every product must be of satisfactory quality, regardless of price i.e. it must do the job that it was designed and built for. Quality may also be a function of price. For example a paper cup may not need to be high quality.

- **features:** there should be something about the product that makes it stand out from other products of the same type.

- **style (of its own):** not only should the product be stylish, it should also be distinguishable.

- **a range of sizes:** to cater for different market segments. This is particularly important in the clothing industry. There is nothing more frustrating to a consumer than not being able to purchase a product because of restrictions in size.

- **backup service to assist customers:** with the increasing complexity of technical products in the 21st century, backup service is important to the consumer, either by telephone or fax.

- **warranties (implied or written):** all products have a warranty. Even a small inexpensive item has an implied warranty that it will do the job it is designed to do. Expensive items such as cars and houses will have a written warranty.
- **returnable if faulty:** as in the case above if a product is found to be faulty it can be returned for either a new one, a refund or credit on future purchases.
- **positioning**: this is a key aspect of the marketing mix. It's the image a product has in the mind of a consumer. Products can be positioned in the market according to price and quality, image, target market or its competition. For example "No Frills" brand of grocery lines are positioned at the lower end of the market, some cars are positioned according to image and target market.

Price and pricing methods

This is something that the marketer must consider very carefully. If the price of a product is set too high, sales will be slow, if it is set too low sales will be faster but break even may be too difficult to achieve.

Price must be in line with the value of the product or consumers will purchase the competitors products. There are several types of price concepts:

- **Cost pricing:** This is sometimes known as "cost price plus a margin". This method of pricing is the traditional and also most common method. The selling price is obtained by adding an explicit profit margin to the total cost of an item e.g. a music store buys CD's from a manufacturer for $15 and adds a mark up of $10 to make the selling price $25. The selling price in this case will be determined by the level of profit is required by the retailer.
- **Market pricing:** This occurs where a business prices their product according to what the business feels the market can pay. A good example of this often occurs in say the restaurant industry when certain "exclusive" restaurants feel that they can charge very high prices for meals and the accompanying service. If the public (market) doesn't think that they are worth it then that restaurant will have to reduce prices or risk going out of business.
- **Competitive pricing:** This occurs when prices are set in relation to competitors prices. Here a producer sets their prices according to the prices of their competitors. Often if a business sets its price way above its competitors then they will lose business and market share. This is important in the airline industry where the service (flying someone from point A to point B) is an undifferentiated product. For example the experience on Virgin Blue is much the same as that on QANTAS, Jet Star or Tiger Airlines.

Satisfaction often comes from cheap air fares.

However, if one competitor has a large share of the market and their product is different say in quality then they can charge higher prices than their competitors. In this case they will become the "price leader" and other businesses will have to follow them. The other businesses will become a "price taker"

In addition to the pricing methods used above, there are several other **pricing strategies** used by business and these include:

- **Price skimming:** This can be applied to a new product that is attractive and which little or no competition. A high price can be charged initially, but can only be maintained over the short term because the high price will attract competitors into the market and the new competition will force the price downwards.
- **Penetration pricing:** This involves charging a very low price initially to generate high volume sales and gain market share. It is used to establish customers that will be loyal to the product in the long term.
- **Loss leaders:** A loss leader is a product sold at a low price (at cost or below cost) to stimulate other profitable sales. One use of a loss leader is to draw **customers** into a store where they are likely to buy other goods. The vendor expects that the typical customer will purchase other items at the same time as the loss leader and that the profit made on these items will be such that an overall profit is generated for the vendor.

An example is a **supermarket** selling **sugar** or **milk** at less than cost to draw customers to that particular supermarket. Indeed this was a ploy used by Coles and followed by Woolworths at the start of 2011.

When motor vehicle dealerships use this practice, they offer at least one vehicle below cost. If the loss leader vehicle has been sold, the salesperson then tries to sell another vehicle at the regular price. A customer who has missed the loss leading vehicle is unlikely to find a better deal elsewhere. This practice can be seen as a form of deceptive advertising (known as 'bait and switch' advertising and is an illegal and unethical marketing practice.

Characteristics of loss leaders

- A loss leader may be placed in an inconvenient part of the store, so that purchasers must walk past other goods which have higher **profit margins.**
- A loss leader is usually a product that customers purchase frequently- thus they are aware of its usual price and that a lower price is a bargain.
- Loss leaders are often scarce, to discourage stockpiling. The seller must use this technique regularly if he expects his customers to come back.
- The retailer will often limit how much a customer can buy.
- Some loss leader items are perishable, and thus can't be stockpiled.

Some examples of typical loss leaders include milk (discussed above), eggs, **rice**, and other inexpensive items that grocers wouldn't want to sell without other purchases.

Inkjet and **laser printers** are also often sold to retail customers below their margin price and could also be viewed as loss leaders. Some of the printers, especially the entry-level models, are sold at a loss-leading price which seems apparently affordable to most consumers, but they pay the regular price for ink cartridges or toner, and specialty papers supplied by the manufacturer. The manufacturer also limits the customers' options by not supporting third party ink, including refills. This analysis more closely parallels the strategies of tying and bundling products, however.

Mobile phones are offered for free or at a low cost to subscribers who enter into a contract that is typically between 12 and 24 months. The carriers profit by retaining customers for a longer period of time, and this offsets the cost of the device. However, early termination fees on contracts, sometimes more than the retail cost of the phone, allow carriers to make a profit even if a subscriber leaves. These artificially lowered prices make it difficult for those selling standalone devices and unlocked handsets to compete.

Video game consoles have often been sold at a loss while software and accessory sales are highly profitable to the console manufacturer. In the current generation of consoles; both **Sony** and **Microsoft** have sold their consoles, the **Playstation 3** and **Xbox 360**, respectively, at a loss and made up for it through game software and accessory profits. For this reason, console manufacturers aggressively protect their profit margin against piracy by pursuing legal action against carriers of **modchips** and **jailbreaks**.

Price points

These are points where the price of a product is at its optimum i.e. at the point where a retailer will sell most of their products for maximum profit. Ideally, a retailer wants to hit the point of perfect balance, where consumers view a price as fair and expected, and demand for a product continues to remain consistent. If a price point is too high, demand can slacken, leading to fewer units sold, and eventually pushing the margin too thin such that the company would have made more money at the lower price point. Low prices can drive demand higher, creating profits on volume, rather than on individual items, a tactic used by bulk and discount retailers. In other words lower prices with a small profit margin is made up for by much higher sales volume. It is a bit of a juggling act between lifting prices to increase profits or selling more at a lower price and making money on the increased volume of sales.

These aren't the only pricing strategies. There is also:

- **List pricing**: the price a product is set at on a sellers schedule. This is not to be confused with the price a retailer is asked to sell the product at by a wholesaler. Indeed, retail price maintenance, as this is called, is an offence against the *"Trade Practices Act"*, forbidding a wholesaler or manufacturer from insisting that a retailer re-sell their product to the public at a price fixed by the wholesaler or manufacturer.

  In most large retail outlets, **list price** is now not kept on a schedule but on a bar code on the product which is scanned for the set price. The scanning also allows the retailer to know how many of the product has been sold so that re-ordering is easier.

- **Discounts**: given on goods and services to encourage consumers to buy the product. Many professionals offer discounts for early payment. This minimises the time spent collecting debts and helps greatly with cash flow. Many retailers offer regular discounts, known in sales, as a marketing technique. These sales may be held at any time of the year depending on what suits the retailer. Common sales are "end of year sales" "end of season sales" "stock taking sales" etc.

- **Credit terms:** the conditions of sale for products purchased and paid for over a period of time (6 months, 12 months, 3 years etc). Usually interest is payable over the period, however in times of low interest rates, credit terms for periods of up to 12 months may be granted free of interest as a marketing ploy to encourage buyers.

- **Payment period:** as outlined above may vary according to the amount borrowed and may be free of interest for short periods or attract interest for longer periods and when the amount is substantial.

- **Promotional pricing:** involves a temporary reduction in price on a number of products on offer designed to increase sales in the short term and give the retail outlet a boost. The retailer hopes that boost will then continue. For example in 2011 Coles (followed by Woolworths) reduced the price of home brand milk to $1 a litre in order to boost sales in other parts of the supermarket. As we know we rarely go into a supermarket just to buy one item.

Price and quality is important in the supermarket business.

Price and quality interaction

The final area of price that we need to look at is that of **price and quality interaction.** It is important for the seller of products or services to price those products or services according to the quality of the product and for the customer to only expect to receive a certain standard for his/her money. For example, a $20,000 is not expected to have the extras, performance and sophistication of a $100,000 car.

Promotion

Promotion is a marketing activity designed to encourage a customer to buy. The promotional mix will depend on the target market of the business, the size of the business and the type of product being sold. There are several ways of promoting products to the consumer.

Advertising

Most people think of advertising when one talks about marketing. It must be understood that advertising is only a part of marketing and the marketing mix, albeit a very important one. Advertising takes many forms, from flyers in letter boxes and under car windscreen wipers, through local newspapers and radio/TV to national media (radio TV and newspapers). The type of advertising will depend on the size of the business and its target market. A local butcher shop will advertise differently to a large multi-national corporation.

Personal selling and relationship marketing

This occurs when a sales person tries to make a sale by demonstrating a product to the customer personally. This is a fairly flexible method of selling because the sales methods can be varied according to the type of customer and type of product being sold. Personal selling requires special skill in dealing with customers. All too often complaints are made regarding the poor sales techniques of the salesperson who doesn't have the skills to deal with the customers. When selling a product personally, sales person must develop a relationship with a customer. This relationship might be brief and in very little depth such as when selling cleaning materials in a supermarket or more personal and in more depth such as when selling a new car to a customer or the selling of a house by a real estate agent.

This concept was discussed earlier but it is important to consider it again here in this context. Marketers must have a good relationship with their customers and this is where the term **relationship marketing** comes in. **Relationship marketing** is the developing of a personal relationship with customers as a way of marketing a product.

Focus Point

Relationship marketing is the developing of a personal relationship with customers as a way of marketing a product.

Customers demand a high level of service. Products such as soap, toothpaste or salt don't require a service to go with them, but a service is required with a more expensive product such as a motor vehicle and this service enhances the appeal of the product to the consumer. Also, an offer may consist of a major service with accompanying minor goods or services. For example, airline passengers are buying a transport service—they arrive at their destination without anything tangible to show for their expenditure. However the trip may include some tangibles such as food and drinks.

Therefore, in summary, an airline company, real estate agency or motor vehicle company must be aware of the relationship that should exist between themselves and their customers. Finally as part of this customer orientation and relationship marketing businesses must use regular feedback from their customers to ensure that they are meeting all the needs of those customers and to ensure that they orient themselves towards customer satisfaction and in turn increased sales and greater profits.

A good example of this is the car dealership that sends movie invitations out to good customers or telephones after the vehicle has been serviced to see if the customer is happy with that service. Real estate agents often send Christmas cards to previous clients in order to keep the relationship going.

Sales promotions

This is a form of personal selling where a business takes the product to the customer is and demonstrates it. Sales promotions may take several different forms. There is the large scale promotion undertaken by a large business at a trade fair such as the motor show, the computer show, sports and leisure show etc. In each case the producer demonstrates his/her wares in an area set aside for that particular business while potential customers walk by and observe demonstrations. These potential customers may be members of the trade or members of the public, depending on the market the business is trying to sell to. Some large companies marketing internationally, send trade delegations overseas to international trade shows to demonstrate their products to the overseas markets.

Focus Point

A sales promotion is a form of personal selling where a business takes the product to the customer is and demonstrates it.

In the case of computers, sales promotions are aimed at both segments of the market at different times of the year.

Sales promotions are also undertaken in places such as supermarkets for food products. When the customer tastes a sample of the product, they are more likely to buy. Competitions and short-term discount periods are also a major form of sales promotion.

Publicity, public relations and the communication process

This is any form of letting the customer know that a product exists and can involve any of the above promotional methods. In addition publicity may involve such things as testimonial letters, word of mouth information and sponsorships of special events and sporting teams.

The communication process often involves **opinion leaders** and **word of mouth.** Opinion leaders are used to promote a product by promoting it in written form or verbally. Opinion leaders include well known identities such as sports personalities or indeed any well known person who is willing to put their name against a product as a way of promoting or endorsing it.

The importance of word of mouth is often overlooked as a method of promoting a product, particularly for the small business. Much business is obtained through the good publicity that comes when customers talk to their friends about the satisfaction they have received from a particular product or service. Even large businesses have to be aware of the value of word of mouth promotion. For example, people discuss the car they have just purchased or the service they were given at a particular international hotel. That is why, in the case of the hotel, free nights or free dinners may be given to customers who have legitimate complaints about the service.

Public relations is slightly different to publicity in that the main goal of a public relations department is to enhance a company's reputation. Staff that work in public relations, or as it is commonly known, PR, are skilled publicists. They are able to present a company or individual to the world in the best light. The role of a public relations department can be seen as a reputation protector.

The business world of today is extremely competitive. Companies need to have an edge that makes them stand out from the crowd, something that makes them more appealing and interesting to both the public and the media. The public are the buyers of the product and the media are responsible for selling it.

Public relations provide a service for the company by helping to give the public and the media a better understanding of how the company works. Within a company, public relations can also come under the title of public information or customer relations. These departments assist customers if they have any problems with the company. They are usually the most helpful departments, as they exist to show the company at their best.

Place/distribution

This is the last of the four 4Ps of the marketing mix and relates broadly to the ways in which the product is to be distributed and from where it will be distributed and where it will be distributed from and depends on a number of things.

Location of markets

This depends on the product being marketed. For example a butcher shop will locate in a shopping mall or in a convenient part of a shopping centre. Larger retail shops will locate in several areas of a city and may even locate in urban areas across Australia. Businesses exporting goods or services may locate all over the world.

The markets for high order goods such as luxury cars will be located in capital cities or large regional centres. The markets for low order goods such as a butcher shop will be located in all suburbs and towns in Australia.

Location of a luxury car dealership is important.

Distribution channels

This covers the way in which a product is distributed from the factory to the consumer. For example, a product may be distributed from a factory to a warehouse or distribution terminal and sent by rail, air or road to further warehouse or distribution terminals where they are dispatched to wholesalers/retailers, farms or other factories. From there they are processed further or sold to consumers.

> **Focus Point**
>
> *This covers the way in which a product is distributed from the factory to the consumer.*

Channel choice

Distribution can also refer to intermediaries or outlets used. There are three broad types of distribution used:

- Intensive distribution involves a high number of outlets selling a product. Convenience goods are intensively distributed in order to get maximum exposure.
- Selective distribution involves only a small number of outlets carrying a product. This is often designed to give exclusivity to the product particularly when a high degree of knowledge of the product is requires by the consumer and when the good is likely to be a luxury one.
- Exclusive distribution occurs when a consumer expects the intermediary to concentrate on *their* product or a few products only. This form of distribution is common in the real estate industry.

Technology has had a great impact on the way products are distributed in the 21st century. Channels of distribution now involve the internet, telephone and postal services. A product can be ordered and paid for using those services and then delivered by mail or courier. It is now possible to do most of our purchasing of goods without leaving home.

Local government can play a major role with regard to distribution in areas such as warehousing of products. For example the local council may not allow a particular product to be warehoused in a particular suburban area because of the toxic nature of the product. The council may place restrictions on the type of transport that is allowed to move through an area i.e. heavy trucks.

Physical distribution issues

Transport/warehousing/inventory

Obviously, different goods and services have channels of distribution that use different forms of warehousing and transport. The type of warehousing will depend on the goods being sold. Several different warehouses located across a city will mean ease and speed of distribution, but may mean an increase in rental costs. Distribution from a warehouse in the outer suburbs may mean lower costs and greater control over inventory but may lead to slower delivery. Each business will need to decide on the form of warehousing that best suits their own needs.

Warehousing is important for the efficient distribution of goods.

Likewise with transport. Does the product need to arrive interstate or overseas the next day or can orders be filled with a lead time of a week or more? In the latter case road or rail can be used (certainly road at some point for final delivery).

However, having said all this, in the 21st Century even rail and particularly road is almost an overnight affair. The way in which stock (inventory) is handled in the warehouse is important to the profitability of the business. This handling must be efficient and cost effective i.e. reordering of stock must be simple and there shouldn't be too much stock lying around unsold. That is why many firms have instituted the just-in-time method of ordering stock. This method works on the principle of delivering goods to a producer or distributor just before they are needed. In this way stock (and financial resources) are not idle. In small businesses it is perhaps not so important but in large ones it could represent millions of dollars in unsold stock (inventory). Coca-Cola has estimated that just-in-time stock management saves them $10 million annually at their Northmead production plant.

People, processes and physical evidence

The **people** involved in the marketing process are involved in market planning. Marketing planning is not new. Although being adopted increasingly by businesses of all types, it is still not used by all businesses. As a process, though, marketing planning is often poorly thought out and implementation of its recommendations is not always well directed or controlled. Managed thoughtfully and monitored, marketing planning has many benefits to offer a business, not least in enhancing managers' understanding of marketing and markets, their motivation and their desire to communicate. These people look at barriers facing effective implementation of marketing plans and look at ways to plan the marketing campaigns. Such people are often referred to as marketing consultants.

Process is sometimes regarded as another element of the marketing mix. There are a number of perceptions of the concept of process within business and marketing. Some see processes as a means to achieve an outcome, for example- to achieve a 30% market share a company implements a marketing planning process.

Another view is that marketing has a number of processes that integrate together to create an overall marketing process, for example - telemarketing and Internet marketing can be integrated. For the purposes of the marketing mix, process is an element of service that sees the customer experiencing an business's products. It's best viewed as something that the customer participates in at different points in time. Here are some examples to help build a picture of marketing process, from the customer's point of view.

Going on a cruise - from the moment that you arrive at the dockside, you are greeted; your baggage is taken to your room. You have two weeks of services from restaurants and evening entertainment, to casinos and shopping. Finally, you arrive at your destination, and your baggage is delivered to you. This is a highly focused marketing process.

Booking a flight on the Internet - the process begins with you visiting an airline's website. You enter details of your flights and book them. Your ticket/booking reference arrive by e-mail or post. You catch your flight on time, and arrive refreshed at your destination. This is all part of the marketing process.

At each stage of the process, markets:
- deliver value through all elements of the marketing mix. Process, physical evidence and people enhance services.
- feedback can be taken and the mix can be altered
- customers are retained, and other serves or products are extended and marked to them.
- The process itself can be tailored to the needs of different individuals, experiencing a similar service at the same time.

Processes essentially have inputs, throughputs and outputs (or outcomes). Marketing adds value to each of the stages.

By following various **strategic marketing processes**, one can build expertise and drive your company's revenue and profit. It may take time, but even small changes in key areas can flow through the entire process and produce dramatic results.

Most marketers are trying to do business with anyone and everyone. They are also making decisions through intuition and guesswork. As a result, they are constantly getting blindsided by competitors and failing to articulate any meaningful differentiations.

Physical evidence is the material part of a service. Strictly speaking there are no physical attributes to a service, so a consumer tends to rely on material cues.

There are many examples of physical evidence of a service, including some of the following:

- packaging
- internet/web pages
- paperwork (such as invoices, tickets and despatch notes)
- brochures
- furnishings
- signage (such as those on aircraft and vehicles)
- uniforms
- business cards
- the building itself (such as prestigious offices or scenic headquarters)
- mailboxes and many others.

A sporting event is packed full of physical evidence. Your tickets have your team's logos printed on them, and players are wearing uniforms. The stadium itself could be impressive and have an electrifying atmosphere. You travelled there and parked quickly nearby, and your seats are comfortable and close to restrooms and food and drink outlets. All you need now is for your team to win!

e-marketing

Very simply put, **e-marketing** or electronic marketing refers to the application of marketing principles and techniques **via electronic media** and more specifically the Internet. The terms **e-marketing**, **internet marketing** and **online marketing**, are frequently interchanged, and can often be considered synonymous.

The process of e-marketing is the process of **marketing a brand using the Internet**. It includes both direct response marketing and indirect marketing elements and uses a range of technologies to help connect businesses to their customers.

By such a definition, e-marketing encompasses all the activities a business **conducts via the worldwide web** with the aim of attracting new business, retaining current business and developing its brand identity.

When implemented correctly, the **return on investment** from e-marketing can far exceed that of traditional marketing strategies.

Whether one is a "bricks and mortar" business or a concern operating purely online, the Internet is a force that cannot be ignored. It can be a means to reach literally millions of people every year. It's **at the forefront of a redefinition** of way businesses interact with their customers. Indeed in 2011 Harvey Norman began selling via the internet after having spent much time complaining that consumers were saving on GST when they purchased products from overseas via the net.

Global marketing

Marketing is not simply a local issue. We live in a global environment. Australia has several global brands such as Fosters and Billabong. In order to market these global products, global branding is necessary so that they are easily and quickly recognised.

Global branding

Global branding refers to the use of a brand name that is known world-wide. There are many agencies world-wide that will assist a business to develop a global brand and market it across the world. When we think of global branding, it is not only for the large transnationals but also for medium and small businesses who wish to market their products internationally. This has become more relevant with the development of e-commerce.

Other examples of global branded products include Coca-Cola, Sony, Sharp, Sanyo, BP, Ford and many others.

Standardisation

In addition to global branding, products have become standardised so that they may be able to be moved from one country to another, and so that component parts can be shipped from country to country and be able to be assembled with components from another country. It also allows replacement parts to be shipped across the world with the same effect. This not only makes production and replacement simpler, but also saves time and expense for the product. The motor vehicle has standardised many of its components such that a car built in the UK will be the same basic unit as one built in Japan or the USA. The only differences might be the drive being on the left or the right and the badge on the front being different. This is what is known as 'badge technology'

Customisation

Customisation is the personalisation of products and services for individual customers at a mass production price. The concept was first conceived by Stan Davis a number of years ago. The idea is that a customer gets a product that is designed for their own requirements (different to other peoples requirements) but don't pay a premium price for the product.

Traditionally customisation and low cost have been mutually exclusive. Mass production provided low cost but the products were usually similar. Customisation was the product of designers and craftsman. Its expense generally made it the preserve of the rich. To-day, new interactive technologies, like the Internet, allow customers to interact with a company and specify their unique requirements which are then manufactured by automated systems. Whilst this may at first seem complicated and beyond the average consumer, there are various ways to hide the technical details. In some cases the process will be handled by computers or design technicians who can make modifications easily and cheaply.

An excellent example is that of customising a holiday package to suit a particular customer's needs. This can easily be done on the computer at very little extra cost to the customer. Indeed Travel Agencies specialise in this type of customising service.

Global pricing

In today's global world the pricing of products is very important. Global pricing is a contract between a customer and a supplier where the supplier agrees to charge the customer the same price for the delivery of parts or services anywhere in the world. As globalisation increases, more customers are likely to press their suppliers for global pricing contracts. Through these contracts suppliers can benefit by gaining access to new markets and growing their business, achieving economies of scale, developing strong relationships with customers, and thereby gaining a competitive advantage that is difficult for competitors to break. There are risks involved, too, for example, being in the middle of a conflict between a customer's head office and its local business units, or being tied to one customer when there are more attractive customers to service.

Competitive positioning

What sets your product, service and company apart from your competitors? What value do you provide and how is it different than the alternatives? This is **competitive positioning.**

Competitive positioning is about defining how the business differentiates their products from those of their competitors and how they offer and create value for the market. It's about carving out a spot in the competitive landscape and focusing the company to deliver on that strategy

When the market clearly sees how the offering of the business is different to those of their competition, it's easier to generate new prospects and guide them to buy your product. Without differentiation, it takes more time and money to show prospective customers why they should choose your product and as a result, the business often end up competing on price rather than on product---a tough position to sustain over the long term.

Rather than leaving positioning and value proposition to chance, the business needs to establish a strategy. The business must think impartially about the wants and needs of their customers and what the competition offers. They may find an unmet need in the market, or they may realise that they need to find a way to differentiate themselves from their competitors.

As a result, they may decide to promote a different attribute of their product, or they may find entirely new opportunities to create new products and services. To successfully competitively position the business must:
- profile the market looking at their size and stage of growth
- segment the market into the segment they want to target
- evaluate the competition in terms of their strengths, weaknesses, opportunities and threats.

Product placement is crucial in competitive positioning.

REVISION EXERCISES 2.4

1. Explain the difference between target market and market segmentation.

    _____

    _____

    _____

    _____

    _____

2. Markets can be segmented according to **four** broad characteristics:
    a. Geographic/physical
    b. Demographic
    c. Psychographic
    d. Behavioural

3. Draw up a table listing each of the characteristics and list the components of each. One from each category has been done for you.

Geographic/physical	Region
Demographic	Age
Psychographic	Interest
Behavioural	Frequency of purchase

4. Define the term 'product differentiation' and explain this concept using examples where possible.

    _____

    _____

    _____

    _____

    _____

5. Explain the term 'product positioning'

    _____

    _____

    _____

    _____

REVISION EXERCISES 2.4　　　　　　　　**Page 2**

6. List and describe with examples the six pricing methods.

1 _____

2 _____

3 _____

4 _____

5 _____

6 _____

7. What are 'loss leaders' and 'price points'?

_____

_____

_____

_____

_____

8. Write half a page summarising the elements of the promotion mix including advertising, personal selling and relationship marketing, sales promotions, publicity and public relations.

_____

_____

_____

_____

_____

_____

_____

_____

_____

_____

_____

_____

_____

_____

_____

REVISION EXERCISES 2.4   **Page 3**

9. Write half a page summarising the section of the text on 'place/distribution'

_____

_____

_____

_____

_____

_____

_____

_____

_____

_____

_____

_____

_____

_____

10. Explain what is meant by 'people, processes and physical evidence'

_____

_____

_____

_____

_____

11. What is e-marketing and why do you think that Harvey Norman has moved into this area in recent times?

_____

_____

_____

_____

_____

REVISION EXERCISES 2.4

12. Explain in half a page what global marketing is and explain how it has affected global branding, standardisation, customisation and global pricing.

_____

_____

_____

_____

_____

_____

_____

_____

_____

_____

_____

_____

_____

_____

_____

_____

13. What is competitive positioning and why is it important?

_____

_____

_____

_____

_____

_____

_____

_____

_____

_____

PRACTICE SHORT ANSWER
STYLE QUESTIONS

(N.B. These are simulation questions only and may not necessarily be similar to actual HSC short answer questions. Marks allocated are guides only)

1. Steve has just started a new business selling educational resources to teachers and students. He wants to start marketing his wares to potential customers. He is aware of the:
    - Product approach
    - Selling approach
    - Marketing approach

    a. Select the most appropriate approach for Steve to choose and describe and analyse the chosen approach. (5 marks)

    _____

    _____

    _____

    b. Select the most inappropriate approach and describe and analyse the chosen approach. (5 marks)

    _____

    _____

    _____

3. Define each of the following market types and give one example of each.
    a. resource market (2 marks)

    _____

    _____

    b. industrial market (2 marks)

    _____

    _____

    d. intermediate market (2 marks)

    _____

    _____

    _____

e. consumer market (2 marks)

_____

_____

_____

f. mass market (2 marks)

_____

_____

_____

g. niche market (2 marks)

_____

_____

_____

4. Graham has been employed as a marketing consultant for a large supermarket chain and has been given the task of analysing the factors influencing customer choice of products:

      – Psychological
      – Sociocultural
      – Economic
      – Government

Select two of those approaches and describe and analyse those approaches.

_____

_____

_____

_____

_____

_____

_____

_____

_____

_____

_____

_____

_____

_____

5. Ethics in marketing has become an important and well publicised aspect of marketing.

   a. Select two consumer laws and outline how they are applied in the market place   (5 marks)

   _____

   _____

   _____

   _____

   _____

   _____

   _____

   _____

   _____

   _____

   _____

   _____

   b. Explain why ethics in marketing is important and use two ethical aspects of marketing in your response   (5 marks)

   _____

   _____

   _____

   _____

   _____

   _____

   _____

   _____

   _____

   _____

   _____

   _____

   _____

6. Philip's farm produce business has been showing declining profitability over the past three years and he is worried about the situation. Outline two marketing strategies that Philip could use to improve his profitability.

(10 marks)

_____

_____

_____

_____

_____

_____

_____

_____

_____

_____

_____

_____

_____

7. As a new exporter of sports gear Rupert and James need to consider the various global marketing strategies that they could employ. Analyse four global marketing strategies that they could employ.

(10 marks)

_____

_____

_____

_____

_____

_____

_____

_____

_____

_____

_____

_____

_____

Glossary

Australian Securities and Investment Commission (ASIC): A government body established to monitor and regulate Australia's corporations, markets and financial services.

Australian Securities Exchange (ASX): The Australian Securities Exchange (ASX) provides a forum for businesses and individuals to buy and sell shares.

Awards: An award is an enforceable document containing minimum terms and conditions of employment in addition to any legislated minimum terms.

Balance Sheet: This statement gives a summary of the financial position of a business at a particular point in time. It shows the assets and liabilities of the business together with the value of owners equity in the business.

Banks: Secure organisation which uses funds deposited for investment by customers to provide cash and loans as required. Banks also exchange currencies and and provide a venue for financial transactions. As a group, banks are by far the largest financial providers in Australia.

Benchmarking refers to the establishment points of reference from which quality or excellence is measured.

Bills of exchange: (see commercial bills)

Budgets: Budgets are quantitative forecasts that help guide the use of the financial inputs and outgoings of a business.

Capital expenditure budget: A schedule setting out the planned expenditure on new machinery, buldings, plant and equipment.

Cash flow budget: A schedule of expected receipts and expenditure for a business. It differs from a cash flow statement, because it relates to future cash flows.

Cash flow statement: A cash flow statement is a summary of the movements of cash during a given period of time.

Certified Agreement: A certified agreement is an agreement made between employers and employees regarding wages and conditions in a workplace which has been ratified and approved by an appropriate tribunal or commission.

Commercial bills: These are known as bills of exchange. They are a form of short term (business) loan where a borrower agrees to repay a cash advance in 30 ,60 or 90 days as agreed.

Communication skills: Skills which enable people to understand each other. If a manager communicates effectively his plans will be followed and the business will grow.

Competitive positioning: Is about defining how you'll "differentiate" your offering and create value for your market.

Competitive pricing: This occurs when prices are set in relation to competitors prices.

Computer aided design (CAD): Design functions are automated by using computers.

Computer aided manufacture (CAM): This is software which allows the manufacturing process to become controlled by a computer.

Consumer markets: These consist of all the individuals and households who buy goods and services for personal consumption.

Contract manufacturing: The practice of outsourcing production instead of producing the function in house.

Contract worker: A contract worker hires his labour on an hourly basis, instead of becoming an employee.

Control: This is one of the managerial functions like planning, organizing, staffing and directing. In quality management, it is the operative stage, and may be used to describe all of these functions.

Corporate responsibility: The responsibility that business has to other businesses and the community generally.

Cost centre: A cost centre is a location, function or items of equipment monitored to determine operating costs for control purposes.

Cost control: Cost control involves careful purchasing, minimizing waste and efficient inventory control.

Cost leadership: This is an operating policy producing goods or services at the lowest cost possible to the business. Lower costs maximises profits, enabling business to establish a competitive advantage over its competitors.

Cost pricing: Selling goods at the producer's historical cost, i.e without making a profit.

Credit terms: These are the conditions of sale setting out how goods will be paid for, and the time to pay (30, 60 or 90 days).

Current assets: Consist of assets that can be turned into cash in a short period of time (usually within the accounting period). Current assets include cash, accounts receivable, inventories (which can be turned to cash quickly) and cash paid in advance.

Current liabilities: These are liabilities that may be called on in the short term (within one accounting period) and include accounts payable and overdrafts.

Customer orientation: When identifying consumer needs the marketer must identify what the consumer wants.

Customisation: Is the personalisation of products and services for individual customers.

Customise: To customise is to modify something according to a customer's individual requirements.

Data Miners: These are organisations which use huge data bases to pin point consumer preferences.

Debentures: A debenture is a loan to a company that is not necessarily secured by a mortgage on specific property but secured by the overall assets of the company.

Deceptive and misleading advertising: This occurs when, in the promotion of a product or service, a representation is made to the public that is false or misleading.

Demographics: Age, income, gender, marital status, sex, income etc

Derivatives: These are simple financial contracts whose value is linked to or derived from an underlying asset, such as stocks, bonds, commodities, loans and exchange rates.

De-skilling: This occurs when changed procedures (usually as a result of technology) removes a job that once required skill and replaces it with a job that doesn't.

Discounts: These are given on goods and services to encourage consumers to buy the product.

Discounts for early payments: Many businesses offer discounts to debtors for early payments as a means of improving cash flow.

Distribution channels: This covers the way in which a product is distributed from the factory to the consumer.

Double Loop learning: results in radical changes in the way the company does business. Double-loop learning allows the organisation to break out of existing thought patterns and to create a new mindset.

Effective profitability management: Refers to the maximisation of revenue and the minimisation of costs.

Efficiency: Describes how well a business is being run i.e. how efficiently the business is using its resources such as labour, finance or equipment.

e-marketing or electronic marketing: refers to the application of marketing principles and techniques via electronic media and more specifically the Internet.

Employees: People who work for employers for a wage or salary.

Employer associations: advise employers of their rights and obligations with regard to their employees and provide representation at Industrial Relations Commission (IRC) hearings where necessary.

Employers or management: is the group of people who own and manage a business.

Employment Contract: An employment contract is an agreement between an employer and employee/s that defines the rights and conditions for work.

Enterprise Agreement: An enterprise agreement is an agreement between an employer and an employee or employee group which covers wages and terms and conditions of work.

Equal Employment Opportunity (EEO): An employment policy where employees and employers have the responsibility to work to their full capacity, to recognise the skills and talents of other staff members to respect cultural and social diversity among colleagues and customers, to refuse to co-operate in, or condone any behaviour that may harass a colleague. (www.lawlink.nsw.gov.au)

Equity: Refers to the capital and accumulated funds and reserves shown in the balance sheet that is the owners share of a business.

Equity finance: The money (capital) put into a business by its owners. This may consist of cash, shares purchased in the business or retained profits. (See retained profits)

Exchange rate: i.e. the value of one currency against another.

Expense budgets: A forecast of all the activities of a business and the associated expenses involved.

Expense minimisation: A policy or practice of producing goods or services at the lowest possible cost or expenditure.

External funds: are the funds used in a business that have been obtained from a source outside the business. This is usually in the form of debt finance.

Factoring: This is the selling of accounts receivable to a financier. This is regarded as an important source of finance because the business is receiving immediate funds to use as working capital.

FIFO(First -In-First Out): An asset-management and valuation method in which the assets produced or acquired first are sold, used or disposed of first. FIFO may be used by a individual or a corporation.

Fixed cost: A fixed cost is a cost to a business that has to be made regardless of the level of output.

Flat Management Structures: As a response to change, flatter management structures have become more common over the past ten years. Businesses adopt a flatter management structure to reduce the number of levels of management, giving greater responsibility to middle managers.

Flexible employees: work flexible hours according to need. The conditions here are similar to casual employees unless a permanent employment agreement is decided on.

Flexible work practices: These are patterns of work that allow employees to vary their work commitments around the pressures of other responsibilities. They can assist employees in effectively managing work and family duties.

Foreign exchange (forex) market: The forex market is where currencies are traded by financial institutions acting as buyers and sellers.

Gantt chart: is a sequencing tool presented as a bar graph with time and activities shown on the two axes.

Global branding: This refers to the use of a brand name that is known world-wide.

Globalisation: Globalisation is the bringing together all of the world's economies for the purposes of trade and culture. It is the removing of barriers--trade barriers, language barriers, cultural barriers. It leads to the freeing up of the movement of labour from one country to another, the unification of laws and the unification of currency. It also involves financial flows, investment, technology and general economic behaviour in and between nations.

Global pricing: This is a contract between a customer and a supplier where the supplier agrees to charge the customer the same price for the delivery of parts or services anywhere in the world.

Global sourcing: This refers to the action of a business sourcing its raw materials from anywhere in the world. It is also a term used to describe the practice of sourcing raw materials from the global market for goods and services across geopolitical boundaries.

Goodwill: Goodwill is an intangible asset equal to that part of total assets which cannot be attributed to the separate business assets. In some ways it represents the synergy of the business.

Greenfields agreements: These involve a genuinely new enterprise that one or more employers are establishing or propose to establish and who have not yet employed persons necessary for the normal conduct of the enterprise. Such agreements may be either a single-enterprise agreement or a multi-enterprise agreement.

Growth: Business growth occurs with increased sales, by merging with other businesses or acquiring other businesses. In the balance sheet, growth is measured by the growth in the value of the business assets.

Head hunting: Recruitment by directly targeting a key individual who has the qualifications and characteristics that the firm is seeking. The prospect may already hold down a job in another business. The 'head hunter' usually makes an offer which, if accepted, enables the appointment to be made.

Historic cost: is the practice of valuing assets at the time of purchase.

Human Resource Management: This involves the use of qualified management staff in achieving the goals of the business, by ensuring that staff are productive, well-trained and satisfied in their jobs.

Implied conditions:

Consumers can expect the following when goods are sold:
1. the vendor is entitled to sell
2. the goods are unencumbered
3. the consumer has the right to quiet enjoyment
4. goods will comply with their description
5. goods will be of merchantable quality and fit for the purpose
6. goods will comply with a sample
7. services will be rendered with due care and skill
8. goods supplied with the service will be fit for purpose
9. services will be fit for the purpose.

Income statement: (see revenue/profit & loss statement)

Induction: This is the systematic introduction of new employees to their jobs, co-workers and the organisation. It may include on the job training.

Industrial markets: These are markets for goods and services which are used in the production of other goods and services and which are on sold to others in the production process.

Innovation: Innovation refers to the introduction of new systems, new technologies, approaches and products.

Inputs: These are the resources used in the process of production.

Intangibles: These are things such as patents, copyrights, trademarks and brand names and are often difficult to quantify.

Interest rates: are the price expressed as a percentage per annum for borrowing or lending money.

Intermediate goods: Those goods manufactered from raw materials and then used to make a finished product.

Intermediate markets: Often known as reseller markets. These markets consist of businesses that acquire goods for the purpose of reselling them to others in order to make a profit.

Internal sources of finance: are those funds provided to the business by its owners and are in the form of retained profits.

Interpersonal skills: Effective managers are be able to interact with their staff to enable the business to run smoothly. Skilful communication ensures tasks are perfomed efficiently and productively

Inventories: Inventories are raw materials, goods in transit and complete and incomplete work (work in progress). Inventories are expensive and can often comprise 50% of working capital

Job design: Job design determines the way work is organised and performed. The process identifies the work to be done, how the job will be done, the skills, knowledge and abilities (capabilities) needed to do the job and how the job contributes to achieving organisational goals.

Kaizen: This is the Japanese concept of constantly seeking improvement and questioning current methods of production.

Leadership style: The manner and approach of providing direction, implementing plans, and motivating people.

Leasing: This is an agreement whereby the owner of an asset (lessor) allows the use of an asset by a lessee for a periodic charge.

LIFO (last-in-first-out): An asset-management and valuation method that assumes that assets produced or acquired last are the ones that are used, sold or disposed of first.

Line management: Management of a business concerned with acquiring, producing and supplying goods and services to consumers. (Other management is involved in supporting line managers pursue these objectives. Human resource and administration managers would fall into this support function.)

Liquidity: is the ability of a business to pay its short term obligations as they fall due.

List pricing: This is the price a product is set at on a sellers' schedule. The list price is the normal selling price without discounts.

Logistics: Logistics is the internal and external transport,storage and distribution resources of a business

Long-term borrowing: These are regarded as borrowings that will take longer than a year to repay.

Loss leader: A loss leader is a product sold at a low price (at cost or below cost) to stimulate other profitable sales.

Maintenance of human resources: This is the "keeping" of human resources by providing them with benefits such as a safe working environment, good pay and a fair and equitable industrial setting in which to work.

Management: Management is the process of integrating all the available resources of the business to achieve the aims of the organisation.

Management Consultant: A management consultant is someone from outside the business who, for a fee will come in to advise the business about problems with systems and procedures that the business cannot solve on its own.

Management control system: This is a system which gathers and uses information to evaluate the performance of different parts of the business or resources

Marketing: The coordination of activities that determine the product, price promotion and place (the Four P's) for a product or service.

Marketing aim: To meet the objectives of a business by satisfying a customer's needs and wants

Market penetration: This is strength of sales and marketing of the business and its product compared to the total market size.

Market pricing: This occurs where a business prices their product according to what the business feels the market can pay.

Marketing concept: The marketing plan or strategy adopted by a business seeking to satisfy consumer demand.

Market research: Is the systematic collection and analysis of information and findings relating to a marketing situation faced by a company.

Market Share: Expressed as a percentage of the available market for the product. For example if the total market is 100%, the share held by company X might be 6.5%

Market share analysis: This analysis involves comparing the market share of the business with ones competition.

Mentoring: This is a situation where a more experienced (usually older) staff member is assigned to look after the progress of a new employee in the workplace.

Middle Management: The level of management between top management and other workers. There may be a number of levels in a large business. Middle levels are progressively being reduced as business seeks greater efficiency and empathy with its staff.

Minimum employment standards: These relate to the minimum conditions under which an employee can be employed.

Mortgage: This is a loan giving a bank first claim over specified assets such as land or buildings which are used as security.

Motivation: This refers to the energy, direction, purpose and effort displayed by people in their activities.

Multi-enterprise agreements: These involve two or more employers that are not all single interest employers. competitors.

New issues (shares): This occurs when a private or public company wishes to raise more capital and issues a new issue of shares.

Niche markets: are small, specialised markets catering for a small clientele.

Nominal exchange rate risks: This refers to the risk of losing money on international transactions as a result of changes in the exchange rate i.e. a depreciation of the Australian dollar or an appreciation of the currency of the country we are dealing with thus forcing us to take a loss on the transaction.

Non-current assets: These are those assets that are held for a long period of time (longer than the accounting period). Assets that cannot easily be converted into cash.

Non-current liabilities: These are held for a long period of time (usually several years) and include mortgages and long-term borrowings.

Observation: This is the gathering of data through the observation of people, activity or results.

Operations/management: Operations or operations management can be described as the allocation and maintenance of machinery and resources (for example raw materials and labour), productivity, quality, wastage and the introduction of new technologies that will combine to produce a good or service. Operations may also refer to a wider sphere of production such as assembly, batching, creative design and packaging. It is sometimes also referred to as production management.

Outsourcing: This is a situation whereby a business contracts certain work "out" to professionals such as lawyers and accountants.

Operational planning: Making decisions about which groups or departments will be responsible for carrying out the various elements of the strategic plan, deciding what needs to be done, when, by whom and at what cost.

Opinion leaders: are used to promote a product by promoting it in written form or verbally.

Ordinary shares: These are shares issued to investors in companies that entitle purchasers (holders) to a part ownership of the business.

Outsourcing: This is a situation whereby a business contracts certain work "out" to professionals such as lawyers and accountants.

Overdrafts: An overdraft is an agreement between a bank and a business allowing the business to overdraw on its cheque account up to a certain, agreed figure.

Owners equity: This consists of funds placed into the business by its owners. They can also be described as the assets that the business holds on behalf of the owners and includes shares and retained profits.

Part-time employees: Can be permanent except they work reduced hours. For example a part-time teacher may work two or three days a week.

Payment period: These periods vary according to the amount borrowed and for what purpose. Borrowings may be free of interest for short periods or attract interest for longer periods.

Penetration pricing: This involves charging a very low price initially to generate high volume sales and gain market share. It is used to establish customers that will be loyal to the product in the long term.

People Skills: Those skills associated with the management of employees through leadership, good communication and interest in employees ambitions and progress.

Performance management: or appraisal is the process of assessing the performance of employees against actual results and expectations of the manager.

Permanent employees: Employees who hold down a job with security of tenure. They receive benefits such as compulsory superannuation, holiday pay and sick leave.

Physical evidence: Is the material part of a service. In marketing it may be the tickets, brochures or advertising: the non-physical part may be the entertainment of the spectacle provided by the sport.

Place: The methods of distribution, storage and delivery that are used for the product.

Political and default risk: This risk is associated with countries which have unstable governments or those that have a difficult balance of payments situation.

Potential market: is the set of consumers who have some level of interest in a product.

Price: The cost of the product in the market place together with the methods of pricing used, discounts or credit terms used.

Price discrimination: This occurs when a seller charges different prices to different consumers for the same product.

Price points: These are points where the price of a product is at its optimum i.e. at the point where a retailer will sell most of their products for maximum profit.

Price skimming: This can be applied to a new product that is attractive and which has little or no competition. A high price can be charged initially, but can only be maintained over the short term because the high price will attract competitors into the market and the new competition will force the price downwards.

Primary research: This involves collecting raw data from scratch i.e. data that has not been published elsewhere.

Process layouts: These are configurations in which operations of a similar nature or function are grouped together.

Product: All the different goods and services that are offered to customers, the way they are packaged and the types of after sales service offered.

Product approach: The product approach revolves around the idea that if producers produced products and services, then consumers would want them.

Product differentiation: can be defined as the variation between a number of models of the same basic product e.g. a brand of washing machine with six available models.

Product positioning: This is a key aspect of the marketing mix. It's the image a product has in the mind of a consumer. Products can be positioned in the market according to price and quality, image, target market or its competition.

Profitability: This refers to the yield or profit a business receives in return for its productive effort.

Proliferation: When a product category contains many brands with minor differences.

Promotion: This is the technique of presenting a product or service to a customer in such a way that the customer will want to purchase that product or service.

Promotional pricing: This involves a temporary reduction in price on a number of products on offer designed to increase sales in the short term and give the retail outlet a boost.

Public relations: This is any form of letting the customer know that a product exists and can involve any of the promotional methods. Publicity may involve such things as testimonial letters, word of mouth information, spotters fees and sponsorships of special events and sporting teams.

Quality assurance: The QA manager's role is to count, measure and report on all aspects of operations to enable the line manager to direct and supervise. QA reports will highlight any deviation from planned or standard performance and suggest what corrective action needs to be taken.

Quality Circles: These comprise groups of skilled employees gathered together in a process that aims to better the quality of a product/service or procedure that will benefit a customer or the business by decreasing unnecessary costs.

Quality control: This can be defined as the management procedures that are put in place to check the suitability of raw materials, progress of production and product output to minimise reprocessing, seconds, wastage, costs, warranty claims and service problems.

Quality Expectations: see **Quality Assurance**

Quality management: This involves control, assurance and improvement. It is a continuously cyclical process calling on all the entrepreneurial flair, innovative skills, experience, people management skills, decision making skills, communication skills that a manager has.

Recruitment: This involves the ways in which employees are acquired for the firm.

Redundancy payments: When a worker is no longer needed in the business, he becomes redundant, and receives compensation for losing his job.

Relationship marketing: A marketing strategy relying on a personal relationship with customers.

Research and Development: refers to "creative work undertaken on a systematic basis in order to increase the stock of knowledge, including knowledge of man, culture and society, and the use of this stock of knowledge to devise new applications" (OECD).

Resignation: The voluntary action taken by an employee to leave an employer.

Resistance to change: The unwillingness of employees or managers to embrace new practices. The source of change may be new technology, new inventions, new ideas or new stakeholders.

Resource markets: Are those markets for commodities such as minerals, agricultural products, people looking for work (human resources) and financial resources.

Retained profits: These are the profits retained by the business and which have not been distributed to the owners/shareholders in the form of dividends.

Return on capital: This is the percentage of profit before or after tax compared to the value of capital (money) invested in the business.

Revenue controls: These are aimed at maximising revenues received by the business through its business and financial activities.

Revenue/Profit & Loss Statement: This statement provides a summary of the trading operations of a business for a given period of time (usually one month or a year).

Robotics: The use of robots or automation to streamline operations, often eliminating boring repetitive tasks.

Sale and lease back: A device used by business to sell assets and lease them back from the purchaser. This then frees up capital that can be used for other purposes.

Sales mix: This refers to the mix of the products produced and offered for sale by a business.

Sales objectives: These relate to the concept of increasing and maximising sales in order to maximise revenue.

Scanning and Learning: is a process of gathering, analysing, and dispensing business information for tactical (short term) or strategic (long term) purposes.

Scheduling: This involves the time taken to complete a particular job.

Secondary research: Data that is already in existence and usually collected by someone else for some other purpose.

Seconds: These are goods which have failed to meet the design or quality standards of the business.

Security: The charge given over an asset or assets which will be given over to a lender if the borrower defaults on a loan.

Short-term borrowing: This is made up of overdrafts and commercial bills and is normally used when the business requires finance for a relatively short time of up to a year or when the finance is required to assist with working capital.

Separation of human resources: This is the business term that describes the reduction of staff numbers for a variety of reasons, including retirement and redundancy (including voluntary and involuntary redundancy).

Sequencing: This involves placing tasks into an order so that an operation runs smoothly.

Sales promotion: Sales promotions may take several different forms. A trade fair such as a motor show, computer show, sports or leisure show is one form of sales promotion. The producer demonstrates his/her wares in an area set aside for that particular business while potential customers can walk by and observe the products on show.

Secondary Industry: The industrial sector of an economy dominated by the manufacture of finished products.

Secondary target market: This is the second most important market identified as a consumer group for the output of the business.

Self-managing: Employees in a self managed business work in an autonomous fashion without the need for constant supervision.

Situation analysis: A situation analysis is an assessment of a business's current position, e.g. its market share, profitability or competition

Stakeholders: Stakeholders are those people or institutions with an interest in a business in some way.

Strategic alliance: A strategic alliance occurs where two or more businesses work together to achieve a particular goal.

Strategic analysis: Strategic analysis is the examination of a business in the light of long term (3 to 5 years) goals and objectives. It will usually consider budgets, forecasts and prospects

Strategic planning: Strategic planning is long term planning (3 to 5 years).

Strategic thinking: This is the ability to think beyond the immediate tasks.

Target market: This is a section of the public to whom the producer aims his/her products and marketing campaigns.

Teamwork: The ability to work together. If the manager is a "team player" he will inspire teamwork in employees.

Training: This is the preparation of employees to undertake existing or new tasks proficiently.

Variable costs: Those costs only incurred when something is produced, such as direct labour or raw materials used. They vary directly with the volume of sales or production.

Vision: This is the ability of management to see where the business needs to go in the future and what is required to succeed. It is also the ability to see the "big picture" with regard to business direction.

Voluntary administration: This is a process under the Corporations Act. It allows a caretaker (the voluntary administrator) to take control of the affairs of a company while the directors are given a chance to propose a resolution of the company's financial problems to its creditors.

Voluntary separation and Involuntary separation: Voluntary separation occurs when an employee leaves of their own free will. Involuntary separation occurs when an employee loses their job as a result of an employer's action.